Tunnicliffe's Birds

LITTLE EGRET. Obtained from Richard Palethorpe
who found it on the roots below Patangan Hall on
Dec 31st 1961. This bird in very poor condition,
probably due to the very severe weather of frost
and snow. A Little Egret has been reported in Anglesey
from various places since Sept 1961.
WING = 277 mm. BILL TO TAIL = 600 mm. SPAN = 950 mm.
APPROX.
ALL DRAWINGS LIFE-SIZE EXCEPT, THAT OF UNDER WING.

Tail square. Twelve feathers.

NAIL OF SMALL
TOE, RIGHT FOOT.

Tracing actual size
foot

Tunnicliffe's Birds

Measured Drawings by C. F. Tunnicliffe RA

With an Introduction, Commentary and Memoir
of the artist by Noel Cusa

LITTLE, BROWN AND COMPANY
BOSTON TORONTO

Library of Congress Catalog Card No. 84-81060

First American Edition

First published in Great Britain by Victor Gollancz Ltd
Designed by Harold Bartram
Printed in Great Britain

Frontispiece
LITTLE EGRET *(Egretta garzetta)*
'Obtained from Richard Palethorpe who found it on the
rocks below Bodorgan December 31st 1961. This bird in very
poor condition, probably due to very severe weather of frost
and snow. A little egret has been reported in Anglesey from
various places since September, 1961. Wing 277 mm. Bill to
Tail 600 mm. Span 950 mm. approx. All drawings life size
excepting that of underwing.'

CONTENTS

INTRODUCTION
The Measured Drawings

Charles Tunnicliffe claimed that it was Reginald Wagstaffe who first taught him to 'be a bit careful about birds'. In drawing it ought, I suppose, to be sufficient to draw exactly what you see. But you are far more likely to draw accurately what you see if you know what you ought to see – what is there to be seen if you look carefully enough. Such is the foundation for the study of human anatomy in art schools and was the reason why George Stubbs studied the anatomy of horses – and became thereby the greatest of horse painters. And thus also, when Tunnicliffe accepted advice to 'be a bit careful about birds', one of the steps he took was to embark on a great series of measured drawings of dead specimens.

He appears to have begun in earnest in 1939 when he was living in Macclesfield and Winifred, his wife, brought home a pochard drake from a shop in the Shambles, that mediaeval and picturesque warren of inns and alleys and food shops in Manchester that used to be referred to by one *Guardian* writer as 'Greedy Corner'. Before this unusual adornment of a poulterer's rack was plucked for the pot Charles made a life-sized measured drawing of it, seen from above, seen from below, with wings spread and wings closed, and extra drawings of head and bill and feet. The result on one Imperial sheet of paper was a faithful and exact record of everything he could possibly learn about the appearance of that dead pochard drake.

But many of the drawings in his collection were of a somewhat earlier date. It seems that he had long been in the habit of drawing any dead bird or animal that came into his hands. However, by the early 1940s he was actively seeking specimens. He let it widely be known that he wanted corpses of birds or animals, preferably fresh, and many of his friends and acquaintances provided them. Many more of the edible kinds were found in Manchester poulterers' shops. Wagstaffe sent him specimens that came to the Stockport museum and later from York. Gamekeepers in Cheshire and in Anglesey sent him their victims and, when in 1947 the Tunnicliffes went to live in Anglesey, Robert Jones, landlord of the Joiner's Arms at Malltraeth, gave him anything that fell to his gun or to those of shooters staying at the inn. T. G. (Wack) Walker and his schoolboys at Hen Blas were a fruitful

source. Owners of collections of wildfowl, of pheasants and of birds of prey sent him their casualties and his interest became so well known that almost any unusual bird which turned up in Anglesey would find its way to his studio. Friends scattered over the country, too, would send him specimens; sometimes the bird would arrive through the post with no indication of its origin or the identity of the sender. At his death in 1979, his collection of careful measured drawings of birds and animals had grown to well over 300 sheets.

Charles was always ready to set aside other work and to buckle to and make one of these magnificent studies when a specimen new to his collection arrived, before its decay became too much of a nuisance. Very occasionally, when the pressure of commissioned work was insistent, Winifred, herself a fine artist, would help with the drawing. Every effort was made to achieve a faithful and life-like representation of the bird, to record exactly what it looked like. Any medium was used to attain this goal – sometimes pencil, ink, water-colour, gouache and coloured chalks were all used in one drawing. There was no regard for purity and integrity of medium such as characterised his exhibition paintings. Nor was there any attempt at pictorial design, though in the hands of so consummate a master of composition, with so keen an eye for the decorative, the arrangement of the figures in each drawing inevitably took on an elegance that he could hardly have avoided. Apart from occasional vignettes which are not measured (and so noted) the drawings were made life-size and were carefully measured, using dividers. Where feathers show individually they were measured and drawn individually. Occasionally, possibly under pressure of time, feathers were pasted separately onto the sheet but this was unusual. Being made life-size and the majority being of large birds, most of the drawings occupied an Imperial sheet of paper and indeed some of the larger birds spread onto two or even three of such sheets. Although he professed a lesser interest in the small birds of garden, hedgerow and woodland, he was nevertheless equally assiduous in recording these smaller birds whenever opportunity occurred.

This gradually growing collection of measured

drawings was kept in portfolios in his studio and was used for reference in his work as artist and illustrator. Together with, by the end, 50 or more sketchbooks, they constituted his personal library of reference material. Retained for his own use as an authoritative and reliable record, they were occasionally shown to interested friends but few beyond the privileged visitors to his studio knew of their existence. These drawings were, as he put it to me more than once, his 'stock in trade'. The collection was incomplete at his death. It never could have been complete however long he had lived. In some instances, in hope and reasonable expectation never fulfilled, he has drawn his bird on half a sheet of paper leaving the other half for a later specimen of, perhaps, the other sex or a different plumage which failed to turn up. The drawings were of individual birds and he was always interested to note and record the differences between individuals when a second specimen, ostensibly the same, arrived. I remember picking up a sick juvenile lapwing at Malltraeth. It died in my hands as I took it to Shorelands. No Tunnicliffe was at home so I hung it on the backdoor handle. Later he told me he thought he already had ample data on juvenile lapwings but nevertheless I find a few extra drawings and notes of this specimen inserted on his earlier drawing noting fine differences in dimensions and plumage. His interest has gone beyond being 'a bit careful about birds' in the sense of avoiding ornithological error in his work; he had begun to notice and record any little peculiarity that interested him, just as his sketchbooks contain notes of habits and behaviour not directly related to the making of pictures or foreseeably useful.

Birds are difficult subject matter for the artist. They will rarely sit still as human beings can sometimes be persuaded to do. They are indeed not usually approachable enough to be seen effectively without binoculars. Sketches in the field can and do record shape, attitude, posture, bearing and the simplicities of pattern. But for ornithological detail, except in the case of domestic birds and wild birds such as ducks that are kept, more or less tame, in collections, the artist must look elsewhere, to descriptions, to photography and to museum collections. The mounted specimens on public display in museums are subject to the limitations of the taxidermist's art and the scientific collections are of limited use. It was to solve some of these problems of the bird painter that Charles made his drawings from fresh corpses. But I think they became an end in themselves and he was happy to devote unstinted time to make a careful record of a bird that he was highly unlikely to need to use. Indeed, in his later years, he gradually discarded commercial work and worked only to private commission, tasks which were most unlikely to call for a

detailed knowledge of, for example, an immature female smew or a Leach's petrel. But he did not discontinue making measured drawings whenever a new specimen arrived until his deteriorating health forbade all work.

It is, I believe, the custom of the Royal Academy, when an R.A. reaches three score and ten or thereabouts, to mount a retrospective exhibition of his work in the galleries at Burlington House. This would have been difficult for Tunnicliffe. His output of work of exhibition quality was always limited by the pressure of commercial and illustrative work. He exhibited six pictures annually at the R.A. summer show, all invariably sold at the Private View, and painted many for private commissions. Once in a while he accumulated a sufficient number for an exhibition at the Tryon Gallery. But there was rarely finished work to be seen in his studio. However, Kyffin Williams, a fellow R.A. who also lives in Anglesey, was a regular visitor to Tunnicliffe's studio and he had seen this fine collection of measured drawings and sketchbooks. To quote the then president of the Academy, Sir Thomas Monnington, as a result of his 'thoughtful persuasion' Tunnicliffe agreed temporarily to part with his cherished collection and an exhibition of it duly occurred in August and September of 1974. It aroused great interest and the measured drawings have been acclaimed as great art. That they may not be but they are fine drawings of great ornithological interest by a great artist and as such are rightly to be prized by artist and ornithologist alike.

The drawings have been exhibited publicly once again, since Tunnicliffe died, at Christie's, in a more complete exhibition than that at the Royal Academy, and it was feared that the collection would be split and scattered by auction but happily this was avoided and both measured drawings and sketchbooks are being cared for in Wales and, it is hoped, will be eventually on public show in Anglesey. The present book makes available fine reproductions necessarily of only a selection of the measured drawings. I have excluded drawings of mammals, of which there are several (otters, foxes, badgers, and so on) but of the bird collection this is a representative selection of some of the finest. Tunnicliffe, before he died, had agreed to the preparation of his book and he would, I think, have been pleased to have his drawings publicly available in this way, and glad that his many hours of patient industry have produced a monument that is valued and appreciated by a wide range of people of similar interests to his own. At the time of the Academy exhibition he told me, laughing, 'I can't work, they have taken away the tools of my trade'. But he was manifestly delighted that the Royal Academy did what they did.

PREDATORY BIRDS

PEREGRINE

Birds of prey were one of Tunnicliffe's most absorbing interests and of these perhaps the peregrine held pride of place in his affections. His interest no doubt began when he was asked by Henry Williamson to illustrate *A Peregrine's Saga*. In order to make studies in preparation for that task Charles attended falconers' meetings and visited individual falconers and their collections of falcons and hawks. His enthusiasm is apparent from the chapter in *My Country Book* in which he describes a visit to a falconers' meet at Avebury – 'How lovely they were in their immaculate sleekness, with not a feather out of place'. In *Shorelands Summer Diary* he relates how he came upon a peregrine falcon brooding on its eyrie on the cliffs of South Stack in Anglesey and how he subsequently made frequent visits to the spot until the young, or eyasses, were finally fledged and away. The diary sparkles with phrases of excited enthusiasm, 'She looked wonderful in her wild garden; her trim, strong shape with its spotted chest, barred breast and flanks, and wide, dark, yellow-ringed eyes had found a perfect setting', and 'The South Stack peregrines are an irresistible attraction'. Those happy weeks of watching and drawing and making notes filled pages of his sketchbooks and resulted in a series of wonderful water-colours of the peregrines in the decorative setting of the 'wild garden of the cliff tops, where heather and hawkbit and stonecrop bloomed among the rocks, as colourful as a Persian manuscript'.

Every opportunity to make detailed measured drawings of dead birds of this species was seized upon avidly and in the collection at his death there were no fewer than seven fine sheets of these drawings. Four of them are reproduced here. That opposite, and the one on the following page were both made from the same specimen. It was shot at Bodorgan, in Anglesey. It is a female, i.e. it is indeed a peregrine *falcon*. (The male, in falconers' parlance, is a tiercel, and only the female is a falcon). It is described in Tunnicliffe's notes on the drawing as a first winter bird and indeed is clearly immature since the underparts are streaked and not barred. The blue cere and eye-ring are also signs of immaturity as also are the pale buff edges to the dark feathers of the upper parts and the pale tip to the tail. The legs and feet, which are conspicuously yellow in the drawing, are usually bluish in the immature bird. The drawing on page 15 is made from an adult tiercel and the mature characters of barred underparts, yellow legs and feet, cere and eye-ring and the more uniform colour of the feathers of the upperparts are well shown. The tiercel is a smaller bird than the falcon (a usual condition among birds of prey) and is paler and more blue, less brown, on the dark upperparts than she is. The drawing in page 17 shows a juvenile tiercel which displays the principal character of immaturity, the breast being streaked and not barred, but, unlike the juvenile falcon on page 11, it has both cere and eye-ring yellow as well as yellow legs and feet and the pale buff edges to the dark upper feathers are almost worn away. The colour of the upperparts however is not yet the slate blue of the adult male and indeed more closely resembles the shade of the adult female. Probably, following a moult, the adult male colour of the upper-parts would have been assumed at the same time as the streaked underparts became barred. Tunnicliffe describes this juvenile bird as male, no doubt correctly, on the basis presumably of its size, though curiously this is one of the few measured drawings on which no dimension is given.

At the time that Tunnicliffe was drawing peregrines on the South Stack cliffs the bird was not uncommon in the wilder parts of Britain. There were numerous eyries along the rocky coasts of Wales and besides that at South Stack I used to watch the birds at a nest just above the road tunnel a little way west of Conwy. Both these eyries were abandoned a few years later, along with many others on Welsh cliffs and elsewhere. This was part of a general catastrophic fall in many raptor populations due to the extensive use of various chlorinated hydrocarbons as pesticides in agriculture. These substances are eaten by seed-eating birds and pass thence into the system of the raptors that prey upon the seed-eaters. Here they accumulate and cause a variety of ailments. In particular the eggs of the afflicted birds of prey have very thin shells and in consequence are broken in the nest and the brood fails.

In North America the peregrine, or duck hawk as it used to be called there, was very common along the eastern seaboard when I first visited U.S.A. and Canada in 1947. It was much more a city bird than it has ever, to my knowledge, been in Europe. There was usually a peregrine to be seen perched on one of the taller buildings in Wilmington, Delaware, where I worked for a time, and there was a well-known peregrine's eyrie on the Sun Life of Canada building in Montreal, then reputed to be the tallest building in the British Empire. The birds could be watched at close quarters from a nearby hotel as they attended to their family affairs. There were also peregrines to be seen frequently in New York. These urban birds seemed to subsist on the feral pigeons that crowd city buildings but, although pigeons are numerous enough in English cities, no peregrine seems to pay them more than casual attention. Unfortunately the effect of pesticides

PEREGRINE (*Falco peregrinus*)
'♀ First winter, Peregrine falcon. Obtained Dick Thomas who shot it on Plas Bach ground, Bodorgan, as it flew up with a young rabbit. Length beak to tail 19½". Wing 365 mm. (14½") Span 43".
Drawing exact life size.'

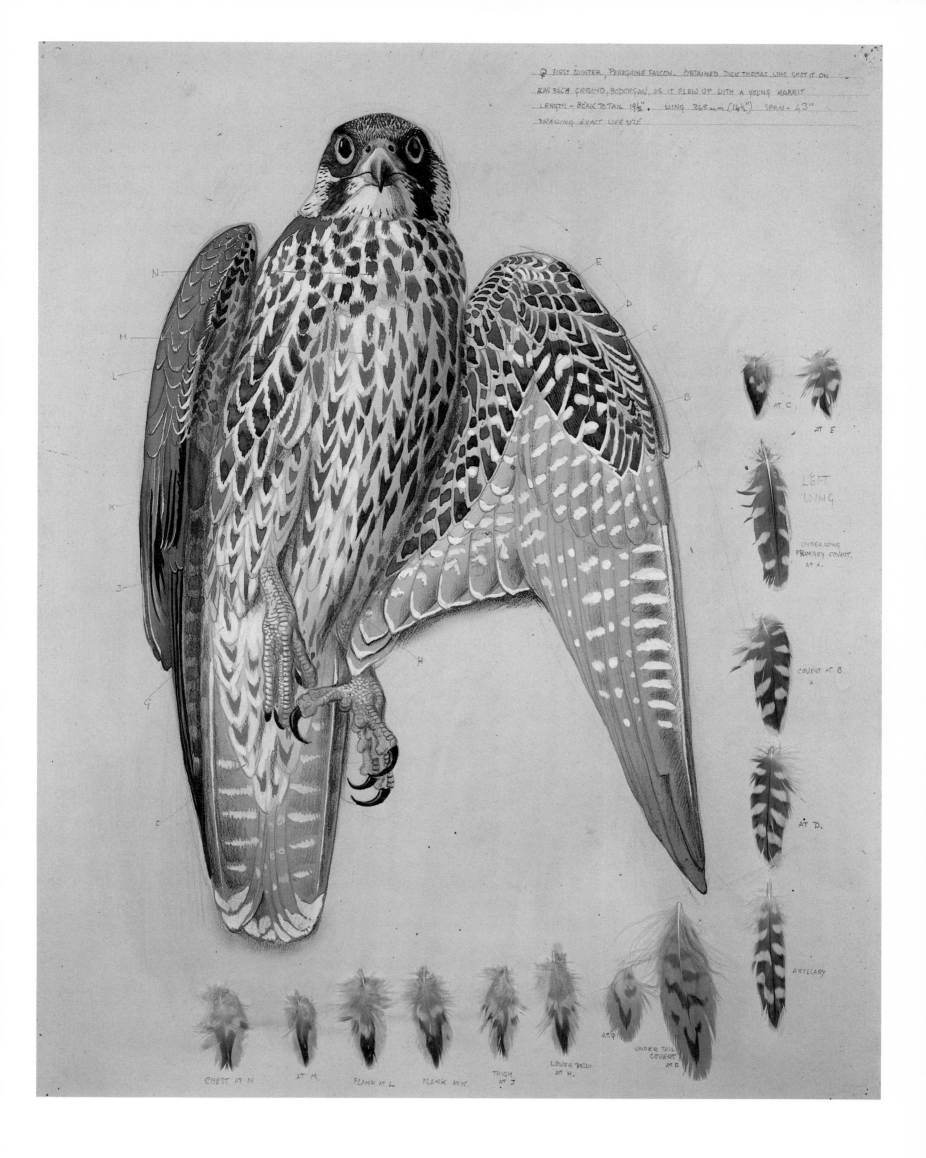

was even more marked in America than in Europe and the duck hawk has become virtually extinct in the eastern United States and in eastern Canada, with now some sign of slow recovery aided by captive breeding and release programmes.

In Britain peregrines are now slowly recovering their numbers but are still regrettably subject to harassment by casual guns, egg-collectors and, more particularly perhaps, by falconers or their agents seeking young birds for training. Many of the old eyries have been re-occupied and, in Pembrokeshire for example, the peregrine has become again relatively common so that it is barely possible to walk for a day along the coastal path without seeing one or more. They are a fine sight. I remember a picnic near St David's that was inter-rupted by a soft thud overhead and a skylark fell all but in our laps while the falcon streaked on towards the cliff. On another occasion a tiercel amused himself by stooping at a startled chough that was innocently probing a cushion of thrift. At least I suppose it was amusement. When hunting the peregrine normally strikes its prey on the wing. This one made several hurtling, whistling stoops but always turned away within inches of the startled chough.

The peregrine, the wanderer, once the family duties are over, is indeed given to peregrinations. It leaves the cliffs and mountains and is found often far away. In winter it is primarily a bird of estuaries, frequenting the places where wildfowl and waders congregate in large numbers. It must be from such wanderings that it earned its name, though it is hardly more given to travel than many another raptor species. The merlin for example, will scarcely be found at all in winter on the then birdless moors and dunes of its breeding stations, but, like the peregrine, will be seen hunting over more fruitful shores and marshes.

The origin of the word 'peregrine' seems lost in antiquity. It is said to have begun with Albertus Magnus in the 13th century. Willughby (1678) seems unsure. He says 'It took its name either from passing out of one country into another, or because it is not known where it builds, its nest having not been anywhere found', an improbable statement having regard to the mediaeval popularity of falconry. The word 'tiercel' is also interesting. It is applied by falconers to the male of any species of falcon or hawk and is variously supposed to refer to the male being one third smaller than the female or, less probably, to a belief that in a brood of three the bird from the third laid egg is small and male.

PEREGRINE (*Falco peregrinus*)
'Peregrine falcon. ♀ First winter. Obtained Dick Thomas on
Plas Bach ground. This bird shot while flying with a young
rabbit in its claws. Shot Nov. 15th. Drawn 18th and 19th.
N.B. New plumage feathers at lower rump.'

PEREGRINE *(Falco peregrinus)*
'♂ Peregrine from Mr Pearson, Tushington, Cheshire, March 18th.'

♂ Peregrine. from Dr Pearson Tushington, Cheshire.
March.13.

15

PEREGRINE *(Falco peregrinus)*
'Peregrine Falcon Juvenile ♂. Caught in a pole trap,
Bodorgan. October 14th '48. Drawn October 15th, 16th,
17th. (Obtained Dick Thomas). Owing to its struggles in the
trap its right leg was smashed and some feathers were
missing from throat, upper tail coverts, etc. All drawings
exact life size except where stated otherwise.'

GYRFALCON

The drawings on pages 19 and 21 are two out of three fine drawings that Tunnicliffe made from the corpse of a juvenile gyrfalcon that was shot in Anglesey in January. From the inscription on the third drawing (not reproduced here) it is apparent that the specimen came to him from T. G. Walker of Hen Blas. That it is a juvenile bird is obvious from the pale tips to the feathers of the upper parts and from the pale blue-grey colour of the legs, feet, cere and orbital skin. These parts are yellow in the adult. Tunnicliffe has dubbed the bird a Greenland falcon but it would not now, I believe, be regarded as possible certainly to say where an individual had originated. *Falco rusticolus* was at one time divided into several races, or sub-species, the name *gyrfalcon* being restricted to the Continental birds and those from Iceland and Greenland being known respectively as Iceland and Greenland falcons. However it is now known that birds from various breeding localities overlap in measurement and that they may be dark or light in colour from the same region and even from the same brood. It seems nevertheless to be generally true that the palest, sometimes almost white birds, come from the more northerly parts of the species' Holarctic range.

The gyrfalcon is a very scarce visitor to temperate Europe, perhaps rather less so in eastern North America. Many of the adult visitors to Britain are the very white ones which are the more common in northern Greenland and perhaps are more given to moving south in winter than are the darker birds that predominate in less harsh winter climates. Although a larger and more magnificent bird than the peregrine the gyrfalcon is not as popular among falconers. Unlike the peregrine it will not readily 'wait on' i.e. fly above man and dog until suitable prey is flushed. This is doubtless because in the wild state it hunts usually by skimming rapidly close to the ground and taking its prey either in a quick snatch as it rises before it or in a fast low-level pursuit. Thus the falconer is denied the sight of the spectacular 'stoop' of the peregrine at birds high in the air that provides so much excitement when working with this species. Nevertheless, in mediaeval times, the gyrfalcon seems to have been a favourite falcon and to own this bird was accounted a mark and privilege of royalty.

Tunnicliffe made a series of sketches in 1951 of a gyrfalcon trained to falconry that belonged to Ronald Stevens. Some of these are reproduced in *Sketches of Bird Life* (plates 56 and 57). From these, and aided no doubt by the measured drawings reproduced here, he developed a fine watercolour of a captive gyrfalcon entitled 'The One from Norway'.

GYRFALCON (*Falco rusticolus*)
'Jan. 11th. Juvenile Greenland falcon. Length 23" (585 mm) Wing 415 mm. Weight 3½ lb.'

GYRFALCON *(Falco rusticolus)*
'Greenland falcon (juvenile). All tips of tail feathers much
abraded. Left centre tail feather missing.'

2ND PRIMARY
DISPLACED TO SHEW
INNER WEB.

RIGHT CENTRE
FEATHER

ALL TIPS OF TAIL FEATHERS
MUCH ABRADED. LEFT CENTRE
TAIL-FEATHER MISSING.

GREENLAND FALCON. (Juvenile)

KESTREL

The kestrel is now the most common of birds of prey in Britain and it was probably always the most conspicuous from its frequent habit of hovering motionless in the air as it scans the ground beneath for the rodents, insects and other small fry that constitute its prey. From this practice comes the local name 'windhover' which is still in occasional use. The word 'kestrel' is less obvious in its derivation. It seems clearly related to the French 'crécerelle' and is said to derive, onomatopoeically, from the cry of the bird. On the other hand Willughby (1678) states firmly, if improbably, that it is derived from a Greek word meaning millet, the bird being 'marked or mottled like millet seed'!

Be this as it may the kestrel is very well known and seems to have suffered relatively little from persecution and pesticides. Although there was a diminution in the population at the time of the greatest use of chlorinated hydrocarbons as pesticides this seems to have been relatively slight. Indeed in recent years one would guess that there has been an increase in kestrel numbers probably in part due to the extension of road verges as country lanes have been superseded by motorways. These grassy and undisturbed expanses no doubt harbour numbers of the short-tailed vole that constitutes the kestrel's main quarry. Certainly one rarely drives far along a motorway without seeing one of these birds performing its extraordinarily skilful and unmatched trick, hanging quite stationary, head to wind, apparently without effort. Other birds may hover but none so elegantly as this. Buzzards, particularly rough-legged buzzards, are much given to hovering, if the wind be right, but the operation is relatively brief and wears something of the air of a tiresome struggle. The American kestrel (*Falco sparverius*), formerly known as the sparrowhawk, is a very similar bird and it too hunts to some extent by hovering, though to judge from the frequency with which one sees it perched watchfully on telegraph poles, wires, or on tree branches, I doubt that hovering is its preferred technique. The European kestrel will, of course, hunt from a perch, but is comparatively rarely seen on roadside posts and wires. Kestrels frequent the water-meadows by my home and if these be typical, hunting from a perch is by no means rare. I often see a kestrel sitting on one of the branches of a few sycamore trees in the meadow. They sit in such places quietly for minutes at a time before either gliding away or dropping neatly onto some edible morsel which they usually carry back to their perch.

Tunnicliffe had four sheets of drawings of kestrels, two were made from adult male birds, one from an adult female and one from a juvenile male. We reproduce one of the drawings of a male and also that of the adult female. The adult male with its red back and wings and blue head and blue, black-barred tail is a very striking and unmistakable bird. The brown female is, as is usual among birds of prey, somewhat the larger and she is far less distinctive.

KESTREL (*Falco tinnunculus*)
'Kestrel ♂. Obtained R. O. Jones. Malltraeth Marsh. Wing 255 mm. Span 27" approx. Length 340 mm. Weight 7 oz. Drawn Nov. 2nd, 3rd and 4th.'

KESTREL ♂ OBTAINED R.O. JONES
NOV 1ᵗ '49 MALLTRAETH MARSH.
WING 255 mm. SPAN 27" APPROX.
LENGTH 340 mm. WEIGHT 7 ozs.
DRAWN NOV 2ⁿᵈ 3ʳᵈ & 4ᵗʰ

EYE WITH LIDS
HALF CLOSED
NUR DOWNY TUFTS
COVERING LIDS

MANTLE

LOWER
BACK

RUMP

UPPER
TAIL
COVERTS

LEFT FOOT × 2

KESTREL *(Falco tinnunculus)*
'Kestrel ♀. Obtained from John Ash, Fordingbridge, Hants.
March 1st. '54. Possibly shot Feb. 26th or 27th. Wing
262 mm. Bill to tail 14⅛" approx.'

KESTREL. ♀

Obtained from John Ash, Fordingbridge, Hants. March 1ˢᵗ '54. Possibly shot
Feb 26 or 27. Wing. 262 mm. Bill to Tail. 14⅜" approx.

Several new feathers
here

New mantle
feathers.

Secondary at A.

mid scapular

Upper mantle.

Upper Tail covert.

Longest
Axillary

breast.

upper belly

Centre belly

upper flank

hind flank

mid flank

A

Tail feathers worn at
tips except ↗

Two centre Tail feathers
new. One not fully down.

25

MONTAGU'S HARRIER
HEN HARRIER

Montagu's harrier is now an exceedingly rare bird in Britain but for a time during and immediately after the Second World War it was more common than it had been for a generation. A few pairs then bred regularly in Anglesey for a number of years but they do so no longer. This is part of a general drastic diminution in Britain that still continues. When Tunnicliffe went to live at Malltraeth there were one or two pairs breeding annually in the sedge-beds that border the Cefni estuary on its southern shore and Montagu's harriers could frequently be seen from his studio window as they hunted over the marshes. The bird illustrated on pages 28 and 29 was a live bird that the Tunnicliffes kept for several months and subsequently released. The drawings in consequence are, at best, roughly measured. There are also two sheets of drawings (not reproduced here) of the very different male Montagu's harrier, made from a dead bird 'shot by the Irishman of Penrhyn Bach'.

Montagu's harrier is a southern species and a summer visitor to Britain. The hen harrier, by contrast, is a northern species and, unlike Montagu's harrier, it seems to be flourishing. Although it apparently had been common all over the country in the early part of the 19th century, persecution and changes in land use had, by the beginning of this century, reduced it as a breeding bird in Britain to a small area in the far north, principally Orkney and the Outer Hebrides. But latterly, particularly since the war, this small breeding area has been greatly expanded to embrace much of the moorland of Scotland and northern England. In Anglesey in Tunnicliffe's time, the hen harrier was no

doubt a scarce winter visitor although doubtless less so as time when on, with the spread of the breeding population in north Britain. The only birds he was able to draw were a live one captured in mid-Wales (not reproduced) and that of which he made two sheets of drawings one of which is reproduced here (page 27). This came to him through the post from an undisclosed source. It is a female.

There seems to have been much confusion in the early part of the last century when both species were apparently quite common even in southern England. The females, even now, are not easily distinguishable in the field, both being brown birds with white rumps and of very similar habits. The males are quite different, being blue-grey above and paler below, looking almost gull-like in a distant view. Although they can, relatively easily, be distinguished one from the other, they are much more alike than they are like their females. In consequence they were often thought to be one species, the hen barrier, while the females of both hen and Montagu's harriers were lumped together as a single distinct species, the ringtail. No clear distinction seems to have been made between the summer visitor and the resident. This was all finally clarified by George Montagu whose name is properly commemorated in the English name given to *Circus pygargus* by Yarrell. The designation *hen harrier*, of course, being applied originally to the grey male birds of both species does not signify, as might be supposed, that the bird is female, but rather refers to its alleged propensity for harrying poultry.

HEN HARRIER (*Circus cyaneus*)
'♀ Hen Harrier. Arrived by post December 15th. No information as to sender or locality where bird was obtained. Wing 375 mm. Span. Full out, 44". Bill to tail 20¼" (515 mm).'

♀ HEN HARRIER. Arrived by post, Dec 15.
No information as to Sender or locality
where bird was obtained.
Wing — 375 mm.
Span — full out. "44"
Bill to tail. 20¼" (515 mm)

MONTAGU'S HARRIER *(Circus pygargus)*
'Montagu's Harrier. Presented August 16th. This bird had a
broken wing. After a period in captivity the wing healed and
the bird was released in May on Malltraeth marsh when
other Montagu's Harriers had arrived.'

MONTAGU'S HARRIER (*Circus pygargus*)
'♀ Montagu's Harrier. Obtained from Mr. Roberts of
Langaffo who captured it below the village of Llangaffo. Its
wing was injured and it could not fly. Mr Roberts presented
it to me. These drawings were made on Aug. 16th and 17th.
Feeding the bird on rabbit and mice. A ringed bird.'

These and the drawing on the facing page were evidently
made from the same bird.

SPARROWHAWK

The sparrowhawk used to be a very common bird. Although it was much persecuted by gamekeepers almost every spinney in lowland Britain held a breeding pair 50 years ago. Like so many other raptors it became scarce in the 1960s due, apparently, to the widespread use of agricultural pesticides. It was much more severely affected than the kestrel, doubtless because it preys primarily on small birds rather than on rodents. It now seems to be recovering quite rapidly. But even when common it is far less conspicuous than the kestrel. It rarely soars except in nuptial display and in hunting it dashes rapidly along hedgerows or among trees and strikes small birds from their perch as it passes. It is usually seen only in a momentary flash as it darts through a gap or skims across a road. When resting it commonly adopts a very inconspicuous perch.

Of Tunnicliffe's several drawings of sparrowhawks we reproduce two, one of an adult male and the other of an adult female, both provided by T. G. Walker of Hen Blas. As will be seen the male is substantially the smaller bird and is really quite different in colour for whereas the female is brown above and barred brown on white below the male is a slate-blue above and the barring of the underside is markedly rufous. Small and fierce, the sparrowhawk when seen at close quarters is very striking with long, slender yellow legs and a glittering yellow eye. It is shy of human company but can be very bold and dashing in pursuit of its prey. Recently at our Norfolk home a pair has taken to snatching tits from the bird-table notwithstanding that it is situated just outside the kitchen window. They very occasionally perch on the bird-table but the slightest movement disturbs them and they are off, far away over the fields. This practice of taking birds from bird-tables is comparatively unusual in Britain but it is a well-known habit of the very similar sharp-shinned hawk in North America.

The sparrowhawk can be trained to falconry but its much larger relative, the goshawk, is more popular. These two are the so-called short-winged hawks to distinguish them from the long-winged hawks, or falcons, which in general have relatively long and pointed wings. The sparrowhawk and the goshawk alike have short, rounded wings and long tails, a structure adapted to their special form of hunting among trees and along hedges, requiring speed and rapid manoeuvre. There is no measured drawing of a goshawk in Tunnicliffe's collection but he made numerous sketches of captive birds at falconers' meets and the like and he painted several splendid watercolours of this species and made a fine wood-engraving. The goshawk had been extinct in Britain for many years but has recently reappeared in small numbers though it is not known whether this is due to colonisation from the Continent or whether it arises wholly – as it certainly does in part – from falconers' escapes. The name goshawk is supposedly a corruption of goose-hawk, although in a forest habitat, it may be wondered whether a wild goshawk would ever see a goose. But doubtless a trained bird would successfully take a goose, particularly the much larger female.

The naming of the sparrowhawk is obvious enough in origin and doubtless well-deserved, since sparrows are probably the principal diet of these hawks. But it is interesting that the male sparrowhawk was formerly known as a *musket* from which the word for a smooth-bored gun is derived. This word for the male sparrowhawk also appears in Italian as *moschetto* i.e. little fly.

SPARROWHAWK *(Falco sparverius)*
'Sparrowhawk ♂. Obtained T. G. Walker, Hen Blas. Drawn April 28th and 29th. All drawings life size except where described otherwise.'

SPARROW HAWK ♂ OBTAINED T.G. WALKER, HENBLAS
APRIL 27ᵗʰ 47. DRAWN APRIL 28ᵗʰ & 29ᵗʰ
(ALL DRAWINGS LIFE SIZE EXCEPT WHERE DESCRIBED OTHERWISE)

Axillaries.

LEFT LEG
& FOOT

ENLARGED

INTERIOR OF
UPPER - BLUE,
LOWER, BLUE ON BILL
DULL PINKISH YELLOW
NEARER GAPE
TONGUE BLUE-BLACK

SPARROWHAWK *(Falco sparverius)*
'Sparrowhawk ♀ adult. March 19th. Drawn March 30th &
31st. Obtained from T. G. Walker, Hen Blas. This bird
brought to him by one of his scholars who saw it fall from
the roof of her home and found it dead on the ground.'

SPARROW-HAWK. ♀ adult. *Maveltig?*. Drawn March 30 & 31.
Obtained from T.G. Walker, Henblas. This bird brought
to him by one of his scholars who saw it fall from the
roof of her home and found it dead on the ground.

SPARROW-HAWK. ♀ adult. *Maveltig?*. Drawn March 30 & 31.
Obtained from T.G. Walker, Henblas. This bird brought
to him by one of his scholars who saw it fall from the
roof of her home and found it dead on the ground.

SNOWY OWL

The snowy owl is a scarce winter visitor to Britain. It is found in the arctic and sub-arctic all round the Pole and in summer dwells in the tundra and breeds there, living primarily on lemmings and other small northern mammals. It moves southward in winter erratically and is usually more frequent along the eastern seaboard of the United States than it is in Britain. In the early 1960s however it began to be reported regularly in summer in the northern Scottish islands and this trend culminated in proved breeding in 1967 on Fetlar in Shetland. This continued for upwards of a decade but in recent years there has been no successful breeding reported in Britain although the summer occurrences in the northern isles have continued. Unfortunately most of these birds latterly have been female. Tunnicliffe's specimen, shot at Mynachdy in May 1972, is also a female. The male is almost totally white with little dark barring. May seems late in the year for a snowy owl to be found so far south but it is less remarkbale than it might have been some years ago before summer occurrences in northern Britain became commonplace. When in Britain in winter snowy owls are usually to be seen hunting over coastal marshes and dunes and they perch when resting on hummocks or posts. They are by no means exclusively nocturnal.

SNOWY OWL *(Nyctea scandiaca)*
'♀ Snowy Owl. This bird found dead at Mynachdy. It had been shot and one leg had been cut off when found, May 12th or 13th. Obtained from Ken Williams May 15th. Drawn May 15th. Wing 430 mm. Most of this drawing is actual size except the open wing which is in perspective.'

Underwing pure white except for bars on the ends of primaries and secondaries.

Upper surface of outer primaries showing emarginations.

♀ SNOWY OWL. This bird found dead at Mynachdy. It had been shot, and one leg had been cut off when found - May 12 or 13th. Obtained from Ken Williams May 15th. Drawn May 15th.

Wing 430 mm. Most of this drawing is actual size except the open wing which is in perspective.

TAWNY OWL

The tawny owl is an owl of woodland and particularly of deciduous woodlands. It is far more strictly nocturnal than are the barn owl and the short-eared owl. Consequently, although it hunts not only among trees but over open country adjacent to woodland it is rarely well seen. It is however commonly heard, particularly as it often inhabits wooded surburban parks and gardens. Its loud hooting, particularly in spring-time, is the 'tu-whit-tu-whoo' of fable and fiction that is often associated in error with the barn owl. Whereas the barn owl seems to be decreasing in numbers the tawny owl remains a common bird in virtually the whole of Britain but, curiously, it is absent from Ireland. It is much persecuted by most gamekeepers, as indeed is anything with a hooked beak and sharp claws, almost certainly mistakenly, for its principal diet is the rodents which are the prime enemies of young game-birds. Gamekeepers are themselves, however, rapidly becoming uncommon, and the colonisation of the wooded environs of big cities by tawny owls is an insurance against this rural menace. Many tawny owls are killed on the roads and Tunnicliffe's specimen was one of these car casualties. There is much variation in colour from a predominantly reddish-brown to a buffish-grey shade. The bird illustrated is one of the more rufous kind.

This owl can be fiercely aggressive in protection of its nest site and one famous instance of this combativeness resulted in the loss of one of Eric Hosking's eyes when he was taking photographs at a nest.

TAWNY OWL *(Strix aluco)*
'♀ Tawny Owl in juvenile – first winter plumage. Plumage not symmetrical – all flights of right wing fully grown, but the two inner primaries of left wing only partly grown. Feathers of vent and under tail coverts very loose and fluffy. This bird a road casualty, picked up and presented by S. B. Hagerty. Found Llantrisant, Aug. 10th '72. Wing 205 mm. Bill to tail 375 mm approx.'

♀ TAWNY OWL in juvenile – first winter plumage. Plumage not symmetrical – all flights of right wing fully grown, but the two inner primaries of left wing only partly grown. Feathers of vent and under tail coverts very loose and fluffy.
This bird a road casualty, picked up and presented by S&B Hagerty.
Found Llantrisant. Aug. 10th '72
Wing 205 m.m. Bill to Tail - 375 m.m. approx.

LONG-EARED OWL

The long-eared owl is not a very common owl in Britain, though curiously it is more numerous in Ireland due, it is supposed, to the absence there of the tawny owl. In Britain it is largely a bird of conifer woods, often quite small spinneys, and one would think it might prosper with the great extension of conifer plantation in recent years. But it seems that this is not a habitat of choice but rather one forced on it by the larger tawny owl which is dominant in deciduous woodland. In Ireland the long-eared owl is a bird of all kinds of woodland. Like the tawny owl it is entirely nocturnal and, being also relatively scarce and virtually unknown in the vicinity of habitation, it is rarely seen unless its attenuated form be spotted on the branch of a fir tree, usually pressed well up against the trunk. Its voice, described as a 'cooing moan rather than a hoot' is also unfamiliar by comparison with the well-known hoot of the tawny owl. It is a bird scarcely known in Anglesey and not extensively in Wales. Tunnicliffe's specimen came from near Southport.

LONG-EARED OWL (*Asio otus*)

LONG-EARED OWL (*Asio otus*)
'Long-eared Owl ♀. Found on Birkdale Golf Links 23rd March 1941. Obtained R. Wagstaffe from Eileen Wheeler.'
   The same comment appears on the drawing reproduced above. Evidently all the drawings were made from the same specimen.

Long-eared Owl. ♀.
Found in Birkdale Golf Links, 23rd March 1941
Obtained R. Wagstaffe from Edwin Wheeler.

39

SHORT-EARED OWL

The short-eared owl (*opposite*) was 'shot by visiting shooters' on Malltraeth marsh in December. This is an owl of open country and it breeds sparsely in Britain, but, like the tawny owl, not, apparently in Ireland. It favours wild moorland and has increased as a breeding bird in recent years, probably due to the extension of conifer plantation which, until the trees reach too great height, seems to provide both suitable nest sites and, in the ungrazed herbage around the young trees, an abundance of rodents. The bird is, however, also a winter visitor, and the population is much increased by immigrants in October and November. They come at the same time as the woodcocks arrive and are sometimes known as 'woodcock owls'. They hunt more frequently in daylight than do other owls and may often be seen quartering field, marsh or dune with silent flight, banking and gliding with wings angled slightly upwards as do harriers. Their characteristic flight is skilfully captured in Tunnicliffe's sketchbooks. There is a page of drawings of a bird hunting over the fields of Bont Farm near Shorelands that is reproduced in *Sketches of Bird Life* (plate 70) and another set, made on Goldsitch Moss in Staffordshire, appears in *My Country Book* (page 80). It is interesting to note Charles' eager enthusiasm at that early date, (*My Country Book* was published in 1942): 'They were an irresistible attraction to me, for they hunted in broad daylight and their flight as they quartered the heather was beautiful to watch. They looked like a pair of straw-brown moths, so light was their flight. Round and round they sailed on uptilted wings and sometimes they would see me staring at them and would sweep over to investigate. If I lay in the heather they would descend to within twenty feet and glare down at me with fierce yellow-ringed eyes'.

The feather tufts on the head, the 'ears', are barely visible in this species, except when the bird is excited. Tunnicliffe indeed notes, in the drawing reproduced opposite, 'ears generally laid flat and scarcely distinguishable from surrounding feathers'.

SHORT-EARED OWL (*Asio flammeus*)
'Short-eared owl. Shot by visiting shooters. Malltraeth
March Dec 6th. Presented by R. O. Jones.'

BARN OWL

The barn owl (*opposite*) came from Cheshire but it is, or was, quite a common bird in Anglesey. Tunnicliffe was greatly attracted to barn owls and frequently made pictures of them. One of these is reproduced in *Portrait of a Country Artist* (page 31). There is no doubt that the barn owl used to be far more common than it is now. It is the 'wise old owl' of verse and story. 'Alone and warming his five wits the white owl in the belfry sits'. It formerly flourished on agricultural land, feeding on rodents that infested the stacks and fields and using old farm buildings and church belfries as nest sites, although, in common with other birds of hooked bills, it was frequently shot by gamekeepers and others. It is now fairly well known to be a species beneficial to man with a diet almost exclusively of rats and mice and their like, but there is a noticeable diminution in the population in Britain which may perhaps be ascribed at least partly to the use of toxic chemicals in agriculture but also probably to the loss of suitable nest sites in the progressive destruction of the ancient barns in which they so often breed and their replacement by modern structures little to the owl's liking. It is a southern rather than a northern species, and a bird of open farm country rather than of woodland or of barren hills. It is by no means exclusively nocturnal and may frequently be seen quartering fields at dawn or dusk, or even in broad daylight. Its pale, wafting form flickering in the rural twilight is probably responsible for many ghost stories. Its voice is an eerie shriek which, though rarely uttered by a hunting bird, may well have contributed to superstitious fear: 'It was the owl that shrieked, the fatal bellman, which gives the stern'st goodnight'. Its reputation for wisdom has probably scant foundation.

BARN OWL (*Tyto alba*)
'Barn owl. Obtained from L. Buxton, Henbury. Shot Jan.
27th. Drawn Feb. 3rd, 4th and 5th.'

WATERFOWL

SHOVELER

The shoveler drake (*opposite*) was shot at Newborough in January and Tunnicliffe's sheet of drawings is one of the most splendidly decorative in the collection. The drawings of the duck (*above*) are a much earlier work. The shoveler is a common lowland duck, summer and winter alike. Although Tunnicliffe sometimes referred disparagingly to 'that great ugly bill' he was nevertheless attracted by the bold and colourful pattern of the drake and several times used it as a subject for striking pictures. One of them, showing a resting group in a quiet pool in the shade of rhododendrons in bloom was issued as a print some years ago.

SHOVELER (*Anas clypeata*)
'♀ Shoveler duck. Purchased in the Shambles, Manchester, March 3rd '39. (This bird had been shot at least a week before this date). Scapulars, flank, breast, neck feathers and summer (eclipse) plumage. Underneath there were numerous quills sprouting the more rosy, wider edged feathers of the breeding plumage.'

SHOVELER (*Anas clypeata*)
'Shoveler ♂. Drawn Jan. 28th, 29th. Obtained by D. Morgan. Shot by M. Davenport. Shot saltings under Newborough. Wing 245 mm. Span full out about 28". Bill to tail tip 20½".'

SHOVELER ♂ *Drawn Jan 28 & 29* 50'
Obtained by D. Morgan. Shot by M. Davenport.
Shot Saltings under Newborough
Wing. 245 m.m.
Span, full out. About 28"
Bill to tail-tip. 20½"

Axillaries,

Long Inner
Secondaries
and
Lower Scapulars

TAIL.

Right foot.

TEAL

The drawing opposite is of a teal drake and a duck is illustrated on page 51. Both specimens were shot on Malltraeth marsh, the male in February and the female in October. Both are thus in full plumage which in most ducks is assumed in late summer or autumn and retained until the end of the breeding season when they moult into an *eclipse* plumage usually for the remainder of the summer. This entails loss in the drake of most of his breeding finery and the assumption of a plumage rather like that of the duck. All flight feathers are moulted at once and the flightless ducks become very secretive and skulk among waterside herbage.

Teal are very small ducks, common enough at all times but most numerous in winter when the drake is in the full plumage shown here, freshly moulted from eclipse. Another sheet of drawings, not reproduced, shows two male birds in transition plumages.

As a breeding bird the teal is thinly but fairly uniformly distributed in Britain, rather more numerous in the north than in the south, but the breeding population is enormously augmented in winter by migrants from the Continent. It is the smallest of the ducks of Western Europe. Brilliant as is the colour of the drake's head one has to approach very near to appreciate it. The bird looks almost uniformly dark in the distance, the grey vermiculations of the back and flanks giving an effect much darker than similar markings in mallard or pintail. The female is a brown bird lacking in conspicuous distinguishing features except in flight. The pale eyestripe is obscure and the head often looks dark above the eye and pale below it. The little ducks are surface feeders and dive only under stress of pursuit and then rarely. They swim rather high in the water but often with the tail depressed to the surface. The long, pointed scapulars do not drape over the flanks but join the wings in a backward jutting group of feathers. They are not very agile on land but when disturbed on the water they rise abruptly and nearly vertically and fly off with rapidly beating wings and frequent changes of direction, giving an impression of great speed. They are much in favour with wildfowlers in spite of their small size and are said to be very flavoursome.

The word 'teal' seems to be of unknown etymology but the German 'krickente' and similar words in other Nordic languages undoubtly refer to the double 'krick' voice of the drake. The call of the female is something like the well-known 'quack' of the mallard duck but pitched higher and somewhat grating.

In America the teal is a distinct race, *Anas crecca carolinensis*. The ducks, and indeed the drakes when in eclipse, are not distinguishable from the European teal but the drake in breeding plumage is quite distinct. The white stripe along the side is absent and is replaced by a vertical white stripe on the side of the breast and the creamy buff margins of the green flash on the side of the head are even more obscure than those of the European drake. Teal of North American origin occasionally turn up in Europe although these occurrences have to be viewed with suspicion in view of the extensive cult of breeding wildfowl in captivity or semi-captivity.

Another bird, the garganey, or summer teal, is a summer visitor to Britain and is entirely absent during the winter months. It appears usually at Malltraeth in late March or early April and the handsome drakes may then be seen on the Cob Lake. The male is a much more striking bird at a distance than the teal drake, being boldly patterned in black and white and shades of brown and lilac greys. It is a little larger than the teal and the female, though essentially a brown bird like the teal duck, has a more clearly patterned head when well seen. Tunnicliffe made several splendid watercolours of garganey based on the studies of these April birds that appear in his sketchbooks (eg. *Sketches of Bird Life*, plate 117). It is unfortunate that no dead specimen fell into his hands and there is no measured drawing of this species, doubtless because, being summer visitors to Britain, they are absent during the wildfowl shooting season.

Garganey do not breed in Anglesey and indeed only sparsely and irregularly anywhere in Britain, principally in the south east. Britain is at the north-western limit of a vast Eurasian breeding range and numbers and distribution vary greatly from year to year. In its winter quarters in Africa the garganey is a very common duck and the males make fine decorative groupings, for example among the blooms of Nile lotus on Lake Naivasha, that would have delighted Tunnicliffe had he seen them.

TEAL (*Anas crecca*)
Teal ♂. Obtained Malltraeth Marsh by Mr Eric Hughes. Feb. 2nd 1954. Wing 175 mm. Bill to tail 14¼".'

TEAL ♂. Obtained Malltraeth Marsh by Mr Eric Hughes
Feb 2nd 1954
Wing. 175.mm. Bill to Tail. 14½"

Thigh x

Scapulars

Secondaries

TEAL *(Anas crecca)*
'♀ Teal. Obtained Oct. 5th '64 from Malltraeth Marsh by
M. E. Davenport. Wing 176 mm.'

Scapulars

Inner Secondaries.
(these are more widely
spaced than in Specimen.

♀ Teal. Obtained Oct. 5ᵗʰ '64
from Malltraeth Marsh, by
M.E. Davenport.
Wing 176 m.m.

PINTAIL

The pintail is a slender and graceful duck with, in the drake, a striking and decorative pattern of head and neck, and is much appreciated by all who enjoy natural beauty. It was one of Tunnicliffe's most studied subjects. Beside the two drawings reproduced here, one of a drake and the other of a duck, both shot at Malltraeth in December and thus in full breeding plumage, there exists also a sheet of drawings of another drake, in first winter plumage. This is not reproduced here.

Pintails constantly occur in Tunnicliffe's sketchbooks, (see, for example, *A Sketchbook of Birds*, plates 67 and 75 and *Sketches of Bird Life*, plate 119) and they were the subject of several of his most splendid paintings. One of his latest exhibits at the Royal Academy showed a group of drakes in a concerted tail-up display to a single duck.

The pintail is not the most common of ducks but Tunnicliffe was fortunate in that it is to be seen on the Cob pool at Malltraeth most winters, especially in the early morning before the first traffic. It did not breed in Britain, so far as is known, before the middle of the last century and still does so irregularly and in fairly small numbers. In winter the British population is greatly increased by immigrants from the Continent.

PINTAIL (*Anas acuta*)
'Pintail ♀ adult. Shot on Malltraeth Marsh by Mr E. Hughes on Dec. 26th 1953. Head to tail 21″. Wing 250 mm.'

PINTAIL *(Anas acuta)*
'Pintail ♂. Malltraeth Lake. Shot by Mr M. Davenport on
Dec. 30th'53. Bill to tail tip 23¾″. Wing 265 mm. Drawn Dec.
31st and Jan. 1st.'

GADWALL

I remember once remarking to Tunnicliffe that the gadwall, even the drake in breeding plumage, is a dull duck. I was challenged immediately and this sheet of drawings was produced, and several of his sketchbooks, and I was told to note and appreciate the delicate beauty of the fine markings. Nonetheless I think he made few, if any, exhibition paintings of gadwall!

Prior to the middle of the last century the gadwall did not breed in Britain and was known only as a not very common winter visitor from its main range to the east in Eurasia. The breeding population is still very local and quite small but apparently is increasing. The main centre is East Anglia where the gadwall has become a common duck, summer and winter alike. It is supposed that much of the British breeding population originated from the release of captive birds augmented by some winter visitors failing to return eastward in spring.

The drake in breeding plumage is essentially a grey bird, black at the back end, when seen at a distance.

Indeed Willughby refers to it as the gadwall 'or gray' but this name is long abandoned. The same author remarks truly on the distinguishing character of the bird 'that it hath on the wings three spots of different colour, one above the other, viz. a white, a black and a red one'. The female of which Tunnicliffe had no specimen, is superficially very like the mallard duck, save for these spots on the wing which, as Willughby says, are of 'far duller colours', but it is somewhat smaller and the shape of the head is subtly distinct.

The gadwall must be a very rare bird in Anglesey and Tunnicliffe's specimen of the drake illustrated came from a wildfowl collection. Nevertheless he had some sketches of a pair made in March at Cemlyn (*A Sketchbook of Birds*, plate 61). He commented of the drake that 'The sun made his breast gleam like metal' and 'No white speculum showing as he stood. Only when he moved to the water did he reveal it'. But 'This was not the case on a previous occasion at Cemlyn when drake gadwall was indentified first by conspicuous white speculum as he swam'.

GADWALL (*Anas strepera*)
'♂ Gadwall. Presented by Mrs Glazebrook from her
collection of wildfowl. Jan. 24th'70. Wing 255 mm. Bill to tail
490 mm. (13⅜″ approx). The white speculum is often
completely hidden by scapulars and flank feathers.'

MALLARD

This is the commonest and most familiar of ducks but the drake, nevertheless, has some claim of being the most handsome. We reproduce two sheets of drawings, one of a drake, the other of a duck, both obtained near Malltraeth in the winter months i.e. in the finest of breeding plumage, the dull summer *eclipse* plumage of the male long shed. Mallard are the ancestors of nearly all domestic breeds of duck and it is from the female mallard that comes the familiar 'quack' of farmyard and fairy-tale.

Very much a favourite bird of Tunnicliffe's it recurs frequently in his sketchbooks (see, for example *A Sketchbook of Birds*, plates 75, 81 and 85) and was the subject of many of his exhibition watercolours. One of these, showing a group of mallard resting under a magnolia tree in bloom, was published as a colour print some years ago.

The mallard is widespread in the northern hemisphere and is just as familiar in North America as it is in Western Europe. It has been introduced into Australia and New Zealand and, although in Australia it has not expanded much beyond city parks and gardens, in New Zealand it has prospered and has interbred with the native grey duck to produce a confusing population of hybrids. Even the pure mallard drakes in that country seem to assume a breeding plumage that is subdued by comparison with the splendidly colourful birds of the north.

The word 'mallard' is related to 'male' and Willughby and Montagu used the word only for the drake, the female being called the wild duck. However this distinction has long been obscured and the word now refers to *Anas platyrhynchos* regardless of sex.

MALLARD *(Anas platyrhynchos)*
'♀ Mallard. Obtained Jan. 10th from E. Hughes, Pen-y-Bont Farm, Malltraeth Marsh. This bird shot on the marsh. Wing 250 mm. Bill to tail 520 mm (20½" approx.)'

MALLARD (*Anas platyrhynchos*)
'Mallard ♂. Obtained Nov. 5th from A. Cadman and R.
Palethorpe at Bodorgan. (Probably shot on Llyn Coron).
Wing 278 mm. Bill to tail 23″. Wing span 34″.'

SHELDUCK

The shelduck drawings reproduced opposite are from one of two sheets of drawings of the same specimen shot at Malltraeth in January. The shelduck is a common coastal bird particularly where there are sandy estuaries, marshes and dunes, less so where there is a rocky coast with cliffs. It is numerous in the Cefni estuary and on the Cob Lake. The dunes of Newborough Warren, even although now largely clad in conifers, provide an abundance of sandy slopes for its nest burrows. It is sometimes known as the bergander or bargander and also as the burrow duck or goose, from its propensity to use rabbit holes or other excavations, including its own, for nesting purposes. It is rarely shot, being said to be unpalatable. Like geese it moults all its wing quills at once and thus becomes flightless for some weeks in late summer. At this time it disappears entirely from many of its haunts and gathers in large flocks in a few favoured refuges of extensive mud and sand flats. The principal such refuge is the Helgoland Bight. As the moult approaches the young birds of several broods are gathered into large flocks or crêches, tended by only one pair of adults while the remaining adults make their earlier way to Helgoland.

The bird illustrated is a male. The female is similar but the pattern, what Hudson called the 'guinea-pig arrangement of black, white and red', is less clear-cut and the colours are less bright. A male in the breeding season with his plumage at its best and brightest and the knob on his crimson bill at its greatest swelling is a striking if somewhat bizarre spectacle, the dark crimson bill and the rose-pink legs and feet in curious disharmony with the bold orange-chestnut band across the breast.

Tunnicliffe was clearly fascinated by shelducks and his sketchbooks have many notes of the birds in the field, for example *A Sketchbook of Birds*, plates 77, 80 and 86 and *Sketches of Bird Life*, plates 35, 104 and 105, and he made several paintings of shelduck subjects.

The name of the bird, of course, has nothing to do with the shells of its habitat nor yet, I think, with the word *shield*, though the spelling *shielddrake* is favoured by Montagu and Bewick. It is almost certainly derived from a dialect word meaning variegated or parti-coloured.

SHELDUCK (*Tadorna tadorna*)
'♂ Shelduck. Shot Jan. 21st '49 by P. C. Turton. Malltraeth estuary. Bill to tail 25". Wing span 39". Weight 3¼ lb. (One of two sheets). All drawings exact life size.'

♂ SHELD DUCK. SHOT JAN. 21st 49
BY P.C. TURTON. MALLTRAETH ESTUARY.
BILL TO TAIL 25"
WING SPAN 39"
WEIGHT 3½ LBS.
(ONE OF TWO SHEETS)
ALL DRAWINGS EXACT LIFE SIZE

SECONDARY AT A.

SECONDARY AT B.

CENTRE TAIL FEATHER
SHOWING EXTENT OF
BLACK. MOST OF WHICH
IS COVERED BY UPPER
TAIL COVERTS.

Pochard Juvenile ♂ Obtained from
M.E. Davenport, Malltraeth, Oct 5th. 64.
Wing. 220 mm.

New feather
All tail feathers worn at tips
excepting two new ones, one
on each side. 14 Tail feathers.

POCHARD

The drawings of a pochard drake are those made from a bird bought by Winifred in the Shambles and which Tunnicliffe used to say were the beginning of his series of measured drawings of birds and animals. The other drawings illustrated are of a juvenile male pochard obtained at Malltraeth. The fore-parts of the bird retain the juvenile plumage but much of the back and wings has already been moulted into adult male breeding plumage. Tunnicliffe observes the progress of the moult by noting that all tail feathers are much worn at the tip with the exception of two new ones, one on each side. He also notes, in the drawing of the drake, that the 'change of tone on the flank feathers is due to a closer vermiculation on the upper and rear feathers'.

The pochard is a common winter denizen of almost any substantial sheet of water. Its breeding range seems to be increasing in Western Europe and, while Montagu, writing in 1802, said 'it is not known to breed with us' and a century ago it occupied little more

than East Anglia, it has steadily increased in Britain so that there are now scattered breeding colonies in much of the eastern and southern parts of the country. In the west of England, Wales and the north of Scotland it is still rare as a breeding species.

It is a diving duck and feeds largely under water. It thus has a different body shape from that of the ducks that feed on the surface, rounder and flatter, and with the legs more to the rear and with the feet relatively larger. In consequence, along with most other diving ducks, it does not rise from the water with the instant vertical leap that characterises say mallard or teal, but needs a long surface-pattering run before take-off. Moreover it is reluctant to move onto land where it walks in ungainly fashion in a near-vertical posture.

POCHARD (*Aythya ferina*)
'Pochard juvenile ♂ obtained from M. E. Davenport, Malltraeth, Oct. 6th '64. Wing 220 mm.'

The origin and meaning of the official name 'pochard' seems lost in antiquity. Other names include 'poker' and 'dunbird'. Bewick says pochard are sold in London markets, 'Where they and female Wigeons are indiscriminately called Dunbirds and are esteemed excellent eating'.

POCHARD (*Aythya ferina*)
'Pochard ♂ purchased in the Shambles, Manchester Feb. 20th'39.'

SCAUP

The drawings opposite show a scaup drake (there is no drawing in the collection of a female scaup) and they are probably among some of the earlier measured drawings that Tunnicliffe made. The specimen was obtained in the Ribble estuary and was passed to Tunnicliffe by Wagstaffe.

The scaup breeds in Scotland but only sporadically and in very small numbers. It is however a common duck in winter when it is essentially a marine bird, being often seen in huge rafts, notably off the Wirral coast at Hoylake. Being essentially a duck of the far north the few breeding records in Britain represent an exceptional incursion far south of its normal breeding range. It is a Holarctic species and is found in winter also off both western and eastern shores of North America where identification is confused by the presence of another very similar species, the lesser scaup. In most Nordic languages it is the mountain duck (German: bergente) and there is some uncertainty as to the origin of the English word 'scaup' (which seems to have no parallel elsewhere), whether it refers to the shellfish food of the scaup or to the sound that it is alleged to utter. Montagu (1802) says it 'is supposed to take its name from broken shells called *scaup'* and Willughby (1678) says firmly 'This Bird is called the Scaup-duck, because she feeds upon Scaup i.e. broken shellfish'. This seems altogether more probable than that this duck, so silent in winter quarters, earned its English name from its voice which is described as somewhat dove-like in the male and a deep 'arrr' in the female. In America it is commonly, and reasonably, known as the big bluebill, the lesser scaup being the little bluebill.

The scaup is a typical diving duck with round, flat body and legs well to the rear. It is ungainly and reluctant on land and takes to the air only with difficulty after a long take-off run over the water. It swims rather low in the water and in the distance the drakes appear black fore and aft and almost white amidships, the ducks being browner and more uniform.

SCAUP (*Aythya marila*)
'Scaup ♂. Ribble Estuary. Between Dec. 25th and Jan. 1st.
(Obtained R. Wagstaffe.)'

GOLDENEYE

This sheet of drawings of a goldeneye drake is probably one of the earliest measured drawings, being dated February 1939 with no indication whence the specimen came. It is a drake in breeding plumage. The goldeneye is a common winter duck round British coasts and is also frequently seen on inland waters. It commonly occurs on the Cob pool at Malltraeth where it sometimes lingers until April or even later and may then be seen indulging its spectacular nuptial display which is well recorded in Tunnicliffe's sketchbooks. See, for example, *Sketches of Bird Life*, plate 9.

The goldeneye now breeds regularly in small numbers in Scotland and at one or two places in northern England but before 1970 the instances of breeding were few and uncertain although it had been thought for some time, from the number of winter birds remaining far into the summer, that breeding was probably taking place, or likely soon to occur. It nests in holes in trees and takes readily to suitably placed nest-boxes.

The name refers obviously to the bright yellow eyes of both duck and drake and the scientific name, *Bucephala clangula*, doubtless derives on the one hand from the large domed head and on the other hand from the whistling sound made by the wings in flight. It is a diving duck and, like most diving ducks has its legs well to the rear of its body and in consequence has a vertical stance and a waddling gait when, as rarely, it comes to land. Unlike many diving ducks however it takes off readily from the water without the long run of many of its kind.

There is no measured drawing of the brown-headed female in Tunnicliffe's collection but there are sheets of drawings of both male and female Barrow's goldeneye (*Bucephala islandica*), made from specimens sent to him from a collection of captive wildfowl. This is much more an American bird than European, its most easterly outpost being in Iceland. The Icelandic population is largely resident and only very occasionally is Barrow's goldeneye found in Britain, usually in winter, but is no doubt frequently overlooked, especially as the favoured (though not exclusive) winter habitat of both species is the sea.

GOLDENEYE *(Bucephala clangula)*
'Goldeneye ♂ adult. Feb. 1939. The *forward* edges of the
white scapulars are bordered black. The *upper* edges of the
flank feathers are bordered black. *Widest black* borders on the
rear flank feathers.'

RED-BREASTED MERGANSER
GOOSANDER

The red-breasted merganser and the goosander are both sawbills, that is to say they belong to a category of ducks which lacks the spatulate bill characteristic of most of the family but instead has a long, narrow, bill with serrated mandibular margins. This is an adaptation to a fish-eating life. Both are expert diving birds with elongated, torpedo-shaped bodies and legs located far to the rear, and they pursue their prey by underwater chase.

In the last century the merganser was to be found breeding in Scotland but was known in England and Wales only as a winter visitor, principally to the coasts. But in spite of much persecution by water-bailiffs on account of its fish-eating propensities it has prospered and spread southward and now breeds in much of north-western England and, since about 1950, also in North Wales, including Anglesey. It is, however, much more numerous in winter and the two birds that Tunnicliffe drew, male and female, were obtained in January at Malltraeth where it is common along the coast in the neighbourhood of Llanddwyn Island and is frequently to be seen fishing in the Cefni estuary. The drawings are reproduced on the following pages, the drake on page 69 and the duck on page 68.

Tunnicliffe's drawings of a fine goosander drake that came from the Humber extended onto two sheets. We reproduce one of them opposite. He had no drawing of the female. The goosander is much more a freshwater bird than the merganser and is less common in England and Wales even in winter. This species did not breed in Britain, so far as is known, until about 1970, but in spite of much persecution in aid of salmon fishing it has now spread over most of Scotland and into northern England but it has bred only once in Wales. It is a bird of rivers and lakes and in winter is numerous on the reservoirs of the Thames valley.

There is in the collection also a sheet of drawings (not reproduced) of a smew. This smallest of the British sawbills does not breed in Britain but is not uncommon as a winter visitor, particularly in the south-east of England and may then sometimes be seen on the Thames and usually on the reservoirs and gravel pits of the valley. It is comparatively rare in the west but Tunnicliffe's specimen, a female, probably in its first winter, was obtained at Malltraeth. Unfortunately no specimen of the elegant little black and white drake came into his possession but it does appear occasionally on the Cob pool and in his sketchbooks; see for example, *Sketches of Bird Life*, plate 85.

GOOSANDER *(Mergus merganser)*
'Goosander ♂. Drawn Jan. 11th. Killed 1st week in Jan.
Humber. From beak to tail when flat out 27″. Exact life size.'

RED-BREASTED MERGANSER *(Mergus serrator)*
'Red-breasted merganser. Adult ♀. Obtained by Maurice
Davenport at Malltraeth. Jan. 20th 1952. This bird oiled
along the whole length of abdomen. Length, bill to tail
21¼". Wing across curve 8½" 220 mm. Wing round curve
224 mm. Wing span about 28".'

RED-BREASTED MERGANSER (*Mergus serrator*)
'Red-breasted merganser. Jan. 30th '60. Malltraeth. Wing
250 mm. Span 30" approx. Bill to tail 23⅝". About 34 teeth in
the upper mandible. Many more in the lower one.'

EMPEROR GOOSE

The emperor goose has not been known to occur in Britain in the wild except perhaps as an escape from waterfowl collections where it is a popular but not common bird. Tunnicliffe made his drawings from a specimen sent to him from such a collection. This goose is confined as a breeding species to Alaska and to Siberia adjacent to the Bering Straits and it winters no further south than the Aleutian islands. It is a coastal species and feeds on the shore, on mud-flats and among rocks. Indeed it is sometimes known as the beach goose. Its main breeding ground is in the Yukon delta and it is thus a bird of very wild country, not yet greatly influenced by man. It is very little known and few have seen it in its wild state though it is reported to be heavily preyed upon by Eskimos.

EMPEROR GOOSE (*Anser canagicus*)
'♀ Emperor Goose (13 yrs. old) Presented by Mr Dooly from
his collection at Llandegfan. Wing 389 mm. Wing span
1140 mm. Bill to tail 630 mm. Drawn Jan. 1st–4th.'

GREAT CRESTED GREBE

The great crested grebe, well-distributed in Britain until the middle of the last century, was shot extensively at that time to provide 'grebe furs', made from the closely feathered skin of the underparts which has a satin-like texture. These became very fashionable at that time and by 1860 it is believed there were only about 30 pairs of these grebes remaining in Britain. Under protection there was a rapid recovery and in recent years grebes have flourished, perhaps largely because the extension of gravel working has multiplied the number of shallow lakes on which they like to breed. It is a common bird of the Cheshire meres and in Anglesey it breeds on Llyn Coron near Aberffraw, a little to the north of Malltraeth. Tunnicliffe frequently sketched it and it is the subject of some of his finest watercolour paintings. He had three sheets of measured drawings of the great crested grebe. This one is of a male in breeding plumage. Unusually the origin of the specimen is not recorded. There is another sheet of drawings made on the same date, of a female. They probably came to him anonymously through the post. The third set of drawings was made from a bird in transitional plumage caught in a fisherman's long net in the Cefni estuary and presented to Tunnicliffe by village boys. It was drawn alive and released on the Cob pool the following day.

The great crested grebe is a handsome bird in the breeding plumage shown. In winter is loses its head finery and leaves the lakes where it lives and rears its young during the summer. It moves to mostly sheltered salt water in estuaries and tidal lagoons. The nuptial display is a fine spectacle and was the subject of the pioneer study or breeding behaviour by Julian Huxley. The female is equally handsome, indeed almost identical, and the pair are magnificent in their concerted and ritualised movements.

Grebes are fish-eating birds that pursue their prey in prolonged underwater dives. Like all birds of this habit they have their legs at the rear end of their elongated bodies and in consequence proceed on land very reluctantly and with an ungainly walk. One of Willughby's names for the great crested grebe was, appropriately if vulgarly, *arsfoot* and for the dabchick, *small arsfoot*.

Tunnicliffe made drawings of the Slavonian grebe (*Podiceps auritus*) and of the dabchick (*Tachybaptus ruficollis*). These are not reproduced here. The dabchick is the smallest grebe, very common in most of Britain given a small pool or larger lake to its liking. The official name for this bird is still *little grebe* but *dabchick* is in almost universal use. A local name in Cheshire, *Tom Pudding*, is an amusing reference to its rounded tail-less appearance on the water. The Slavonian grebe is relatively rare. It breeds in only one or two places in Scotland and even as a winter visitor is far from numerous. One of the better places to see it is in the sheltered coves on the south side of Llanddwyn Island where it lingers sometimes until April when many have assumed the elegant breeding plumage.

GREAT CRESTED GREBE (*Podiceps cristatus*)
'♂ Great crested grebe. Obtained March 12th. Wing
204 mm. Bill to tail 21⅞".'

RED-THROATED DIVER
BLACK-THROATED DIVER

The drawings on page 77 of a red-throated diver were made from an adult female found, oiled and dead, at Malltraeth. This is an instance where a large bird had to be drawn on more than one sheet of paper if everything of importance was to be noted. The second sheet is not reproduced. The drawing on page 76 was made from another specimen that came from Three Cliffs Bay in the Gower Peninsula. Since Tunnicliffe had already made detailed drawings of a specimen in similar plumage he made only a single drawing of this one. He notes that it was a much darker bird than the other, many of the feathers of the upper parts having lost their pale edges due to abrasion – and the pale edges remaining were no doubt much reduced. It may be noted that this bird died five weeks later in the year than that from Malltraeth so that greater wear of its winter plumage is to be expected.

The red-throated diver breeds in the north and west of Scotland on small, sometimes quite tiny, fresh-water lochs. It has a very characteristic and distinguished summer plumage but unfortunately birds in that plumage never fell into Tunnicliffe's hands, although he sketched them on his trips to Scotland. In winter plumage the red-throated diver is a much paler bird than the black-throated, with more white on the head and neck. The up-tilted, and frequently upward-pointed, bill, so well shown in these drawings, is often a good indication of identity. Like the black-throated diver this species, outside the breeding season, is usually to be found on salt water – indeed it commonly feeds on sea or sea loch during the breeding season. It is probably the most numerous diver off British coasts in winter and can frequently be seen offshore around Llanddwyn Island and in the Cefni estuary.

The black-throated diver illustrated opposite was found oiled and moribund at Malltraeth in January. The bird drawn, as noted by Tunnicliffe, is just beginning, even at the end of January, to assume the summer plumage and has a few of the white-spotted black feathers that go eventually to form the boldly patterned back and mantle. This is in marked contrast with the red-throated divers he studied which in January and even in February were still without any trace of the breeding plumage although in the February bird the winter feathers were much worn. This is no doubt due to the earlier breeding season of the black-throated diver which necessitates an assumption of breeding regalia earlier in the year.

The black-throated diver breeds, usually on islets, in the larger fresh-water lochs of northern and western Scotland. It is not a common bird. Outside the breeding season it favours salt water and tends to move southward, being found in winter along the shores and estuaries of the whole of Britain. It is a very differently patterned bird in summer, with a dove-grey head, black throat, striped neck and black and white checker-patterned back. The sober winter plumage is not easy to distinguish at a distance from that of the rather larger great northern diver which, although it does not breed in Britain, is the more common around our winter coasts.

Divers are called *loons* in America, a word which was formerly (Willughby) used indiscriminately for both divers and grebes. It is not a reference to any supposed idiocy of the birds but has the same root as the word 'lame' and refers to the inept progress of these diving birds when on land, owing to the rearward attachment of their legs. This is well shown in the drawings which also display the lateral compression of the legs in these birds, a further adaptation to efficient motion in water.

BLACK-THROATED DIVER *(Gavia arctica)*
'Jan. 20th 1960. Black-throated Diver. Obtained from Eric
Hughes who found it on his ground at Bont Farm,
Malltraeth. An oiled bird and very sick. It died while being
sketched. Wing across the bend 285 mm. Pressed flat
290 mm. Length, bill to tail, 24″. Span of wings approx. 39″.
In moult from winter to summer. All drawings exact life
size.'

RED-THROATED DIVER *(Gavia stellata)*
'Red-throated Diver. Received from Ednyfed Davies,
Glamorgan, Feb. 21st 1957. Drawn same day. Bird was in
fresh condition. Many of the feathers had lost their pale
edges by abrasion. It was a much darker bird than the one
drawn on Jan. 12th because of this loss of white edgings. Bill
to tail (approx.) 24¾". Wing across the curve 270 mm. Wing
pressed flat 280 mm.'

RED-THROATED DIVER *(Gavia stellata)*
'Red-throated Diver. Adult female (R. Wagstaffe). Found
dead on Malltraeth Cob by Mr Jones. Jan. 12th 1954. This
bird badly oiled on its right side. Bill to tail 24½". Wing
across the curve 273 mm. Pressed flat 285 mm.'
  Data from another sheet of drawings (not reproduced) of
the same specimen.

Flank feathers
NB. Variety in markings
much of which is caused
by overlying fringes of
next feather

HERON

The heron is a common water bird in Britain and Ireland and is often to be seen about the Cefni estuary and the Cob pool at Malltraeth. It was a favourite subject for Tunnicliffe's exhibition pictures and provided some of his finest paintings. These drawings are made from an adult bird that apparently came to him from the Solway region. They were completed on a second sheet (not reproduced). It is surprising that he had only the one bird to work from and there is no measured drawing of the more uniformly grey immature bird. There are many sketches from life of herons in his numerous sketchbooks, see, for instance, *Sketches of Bird Life* plates 53, 54 and 81, and *A Sketchbook of Birds* plates 44 and 54.

The heron is a cosmopolitan Old World species. It nests in colonies, known as heronries, usually located in tall trees, the nests being large constructions of twigs. In the absence of trees, however, herons will nest elsewhere, for example in reed beds, or on cliffs. It is primarily a catcher of fish which it stalks on its long legs in shallow water with infinite patience and a final sudden thrust. Although usually rather shy of man it is bold in pursuit of its prey and will remove goldfish from unprotected ponds in suburban gardens. The heron, of course, is not exclusively a fish-eater but may be seen stalking in meadows for frogs and other terrestrial animal-life.

The word *heron* has long been in use but Willughby, Montagu and Bewick give *heronshaw* as an alternative and Hamlet claimed to 'know a hawk from a hand-saw'. I remember as a little boy in Nottinghamshire being astonished to be told by an older village lad that a bird I knew to be a heron was a *herring shrew* and there is a restaurant in Cley-next-the-Sea called *The Harnser*. Evidently the ancient usage dies hard.

HERON *(Ardea cinerea)*
'Heron. Obtained by L. Piggot, Solway. Oct. 28th '46.
Drawn 2nd, 3rd & 4th Nov. Wing span fully extended 64".
Tail tip to bill tip, neck extended 33". A to B 18". C to D 11¾".
Most flights and tail feathers were new and unabraded.
Long crest feathers were absent but new black crest feathers
just appearing from sheaths at back of crown. Claws almost
worn away. In some cases to the flesh of the toes.
Unmeasured drawing.'

(unmeasured drawing. Smaller than life)
Feathers usually concealed by bastard wing.

½ TAIL. UPPER SURFACE. LIFE SIZE

White pattern along the leading edge of wing.
(unmeasured)

HERON. OBTAINED BY L. PIGGOTT
SOLWAY. Oct. 28th '46
DRAWN. 2nd 3rd & 4th Nov.
WING-SPAN FULLY EXTENDED 64 INCHES.
TAIL-TIP to BILL-TIP, NECK EXTENDED. 33 INCHES.
A to B. 18 INCHES.
C & D. 11¾ INCHES.

Breast flights and tail feathers were new and un-abraided. Long crest feathers were absent but new black crest feathers just appearing from sheaths at the back of crown.
Claws almost worn away, in some cases, to the flesh of the toes.

UNMEASURED DRAWING.

BITTERN
LITTLE EGRET

The bittern was at one time much more common than it is now but it can still be found, particularly in extensive reed-beds. It is more often heard than seen, its curious 'boom' far-carrying over the flat lands. Sometimes it may be seen in the air, flying with slow regular beats of its rounded wings, a rather chunky brown heron. But on land it is difficult to spot owing to its protective colouring and to its habit of standing motionless, face to the observer, bill pointed skywards and merging totally with its setting of golden reeds. Tunnicliffe had two specimens, the one here a juvenile, and he recorded them with a lovingly careful attention to the intricate pattern of black markings on a ground of brown and gold.

Whatever may be the origin of the well-established word *bittern* – and Potter and Sargent (*Pedigree: words from Nature*) suggest that it has more to do with the other sounds the bittern makes than with the well-known boom – there is no mistaking the origin of the majority of the local names, for example bog-bumper and mire-drum, in the weird, far-carrying thump of the breeding male. The scientific name *Botaurus* seems clearly to contain the Latin word for *bull* and Willughby says 'It is called by later writers, Butorius or Botaurus, because it seems to imitate *boatum tauri*, the bellowing of a Bull'.

Tunnicliffe's drawings of another member of the heron family, the little egret, are reproduced as a frontispiece (page 2). This is a careful and beautiful record of a species which is but a rare visitor to Britain and, being a bird primarily of warmer climates, the odd wanderer to our shores is very liable to be killed by winter cold if it remains into that season, as happened apparently to this one.

In breeding plumage there are two narrow feathers adorning the crown and the feathers of fore-neck and back are longer and are elegantly branched into a beautiful array of nuptial plumes. The black legs and yellow feet are a surprising feature, giving the appearance of a black-legged bird wearing golden slippers. But in Australia the local race of little egret has both black legs and black feet; yet, even there, the soles of the feet are apt to be yellow.

The elegant plumes of the breeding bird were very nearly the species' undoing. They became popular in Edwardian times as decoration for womens' hats and were variously known as *aigrettes* and, very curiously, *ospreys*. Since these plumes are present only during the breeding season meeting the demand entailed destructive attacks on the nesting colonies of the birds. Importation of the plumes into Britain was however made illegal and the fashion died away. The little egret remains a common bird in many parts of southern Europe and in India and East Asia and in Australia.

BITTERN (*Botaurus stellaris*)
'Juvenile ♀ Bittern. Found alive, but in a very emaciated condition, on a farm road by Llyn Traffwll. Rescued by K. Williams who took it home but it would not take food. It died July 8th. Wing 211 mm. Bill to tail 21" approx.'

Juvenile ♀ Bittern. Found alive, but in a very
emaciated condition, on a farm road by Llyn Traffwll.
Rescued by R. Williams who took it home, but it would not
take food. Tt died July 8ᵗʰ   Wing. 211 mm. Bill to Tail 21" approx

GLOSSY IBIS

The glossy ibis is a widespread species that may be seen in southern Europe, Africa, India, Australia and eastern North America but it is only a very occasional visitor to Britain. This one was shot as it rose from the Cob pool. It was said to have been shot in mistake for a curlew, a claim sustained by the down-curved bill. Tunnicliffe's notes on the incidence of light on the glossy feathers are interesting. 'There is no constant local colour except in the case of the chestnut patches'. A more than usually emphatic instance of his frequent assertion that there is no such thing as local colour – as indeed there is not; it is always modified by light and by adjacent colours.

Nowadays the glossy ibis is only a passage migrant in Egypt and the sacred ibis is now found only south of the Sahara but both are much represented in ancient Egyptian decoration. Willughby has a curious passage 'The Ibes (saith Cicero) despatch a power of Serpents. They turn away a great Plague from Egypt, when they kill and consume those flying Serpents that are brought in thither by the West wind out of the Deserts of Libya. Whence it comes to pass, that they do no harm either alive by their biting, or dead by their Stench.'

GLOSSY IBIS (*Plegadis falcinellus*)
'Glossy Ibis. Probable adult male as wing measurement is 290 mm. Obtained from R. Jones. Shot on lake at Malltraeth. Oct. 2nd '45. No others of its kind on the lake at the time. Drawn Oct. 6th and 7th.'
'Wing span 39". Length, bill to tail 22½". Bill, from frontal feathers to tip 136 mm. Wing from shoulder to end of second flight 290 mm. Tail 112 mm. Tarsus 100 mm. Middle toe to end of tail 85 mm. All these studies made from specimen laid flat on table with light coming from left, level with and above table top, except in case of study of upper wing surface, when light is from the right. The gloss on the feathers changes colour according to position of light and angle from which it is viewed. There is no constant local colour except in the case of the chestnut patches.'

GLOSSY IBIS. *Probable adult male as wing measurement is 290 m.m.*
Obtained from R. Jones.
Shot on the lake at Shallowatt. Oct 2ᵈ '45
No others of its kind on the lake at the time.
Drawn Oct 6ᵗʰ & 7ᵗʰ.

Undersurface

Upper Surface.

B

A

Section at B

Section at A.

WING SPAN 39"
LENGTH—BILL TO TAIL 22½"
BILL from frontal feathers
to tip 136 m.m.

Wing from shoulder to end of
second flight 290 m.m.

Tail 112 m.m.

Tarsus 100 m.m.

Middle toe to
end of nail 85 m.m.

All these studies made
from specimen laid
flat on table with light
coming from left, level
with & above table top.
except in case of study
of upper wing surface when
light is from the right.

The gloss on the feathers
changes colour according
to direction of light and
angle from which it is
viewed. There is no
constant local colour
except in the case of
the chestnut feathers.

N.B.
Very long axillaries
which sometimes appear
below the wing when it
is closed: shown as in
shorter scallops.

Scale of Tail when spread.

This drawing
exact life size.

Slightly less than
life size.

Middle claw
of right foot
showing comb on
inner edge

Right foot.

COOT

The coot is a common and widely distributed bird in Britain but it is found only on relatively large sheets of water, unlike the equally common moorhen which is found everywhere there is a small stream or pond or even sometimes merely a ditch.

Coots of the same species are found extensively in Eurasia and in Australia. Very similar birds replace it in Africa south of the Sahara and in North America. The African bird is the so-called crested coot (*Fulica cristata*). Its crest consists of very inconspicuous knobs on the white frontal plate but it is otherwise very like *Fulica atra,* although the voice is quite distinct. There are small relict colonies of this bird in South Spain and in North Africa. The Americans coot (*Fulica americana*) is even more like the European coot but is more readily distinguished at a distance in having white undertail coverts.

Although the lobed feet of the coot are superficially like those of the grebes it is a rather inept diver. It is, moreover, somewhat reluctant to take wing and needs a very long fluttering and pattering take-off run before rising into the air. On the other hand it moves well on land and is commonly seen grazing ashore but it runs to the water for security when disturbed. Quarrelsome and given to noisy and protracted territorial fights in the breeding season it is gregarious at other times and occurs in large flocks in winter.

The word *coot* is supposedly derived from its well-known call.

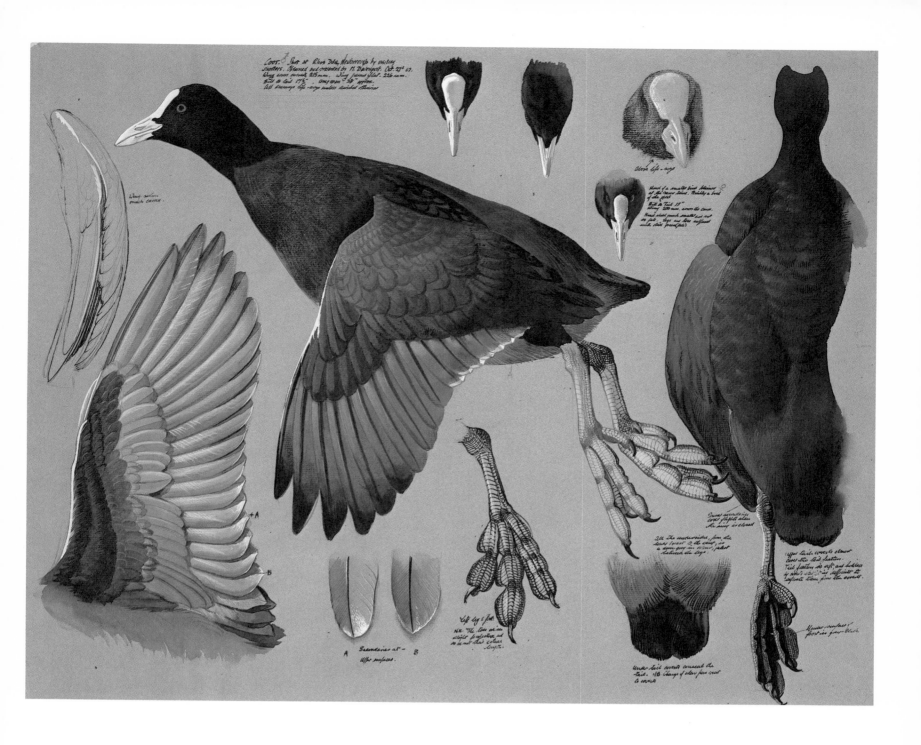

COOT *(Fulica atra)*
'Coot ♂. Shot at Rhos Ddu, Newborough, by visiting
shooters. Obtained and presented by M. Davenport Oct.
27th '62. Wing across curve 215 mm. Wing pressed flat
226 mm. Bill to tail 17½". Wing span 28" approx. All
drawings life size unless described otherwise. Inner
secondaries cover flights when the wing is closed. All the
underside, from the lower breast to the vent, is a deep grey
in colour, palest between the legs. Undertail coverts conceal
the tail. N.B. Change of colour from vent to coverts. Upper
tail coverts almost cover the tail. Tail feathers so soft, and
hidden by coverts, it is difficult to separate them from the
coverts. Under surface of foot is grey-black.'

SEA & SHORE BIRDS

FULMAR

This (*opposite*) is one of two measured drawings that Tunnicliffe made of the fulmar. The specimen, one of many supplied to Tunnicliffe by his friend T. G. Walker, was found by scholars in a field near Hen Blas school.

The fulmar, to quote James Fisher, is 'the nearest thing to an albatross that flies in the North Atlantic'. It has prospered remarkably during this century, supposedly due to increased sea-fishing by man, and, from breeding on a few far northern cliffs it now occupies almost every suitable site in Britain and Ireland. Unlike most gulls which are sea-birds of the coast and continental shelves, the fulmar is a truly oceanic bird and lives and feeds far from land, coming to shore only to breed. There is but one gull of similar manner of life, the kittiwake, and on a trans-Atlantic voyage in winter both may be encountered in mid-ocean, long after the coastal sea-birds have been left behind. They will follow the ship together for days at a time, the kittiwake hopeful of galley refuse, the fulmar seemingly more interested in marine life exposed by the churning of the propellers.

Although superficially similar in their grey and white plumage and marine habits, the fulmar and gulls are really quite distinct. Structurally the bill of the fulmar follows the pattern of others of the tube-nosed kind, the Tubinares. It is made up of distinct plates and the nostrils are enclosed in a tube on the top. In flight, to quote James Fisher again 'gulls appear as high-winged monoplanes with an angle in mid-wing; fulmars are middle-winged and their wing has no angle, but an almost straight leading edge'. They fly with a few flaps followed by long glides on rigidly held straight wings and in the manner of the tube-noses of the southern oceans they are expert in turning to advantage any least current of air. They give the impression of effortless movement over the water that can evidently be maintained without pause for long periods of time.

On their breeding cliffs a pair of fulmars engage in energetic displays and pairs are a delight to watch, billing and cooing one to another and aggressively disputing their ledge with intruding third parties. Tunnicliffe made numerous studies of them at South Stack and Handa. See, for example *A Sketchbook of Birds*, plate 6, *Sketches of Bird Life*, plate 15 and *Bird Portraiture*, pages 82 and 83.

The word *fulmar* means *foul gull* and refers to the fishy odour of the bird and its nest and probably also to its habit of ejecting a half-digested fishy oil at an intruder. This practice is common among the Tubinares and the downy young royal albatross can spit accurately and disconcertingly up to six feet.

FULMAR (*Fulmarus glacialis*)
'Suspected juv. ♀ Fulmar Petrel. Obtained from T. G. Walker, Hen Blas, Sept. 14th '62. Brought to Hen Blas school by one of the scholars, who found this bird in a field near the school. Drawn Sept. 17th and 18th. Wing 298 mm. Bill to tail 17". Span approx. 40".'

GANNET

The drawings on page 91 are reproduced from one of two fine sheets of drawings of an adult gannet, this one a male. Unlike most of these drawings the main figure is a free-hand drawing, less than life-size and thus probably only very roughly measured. The gannet is our largest sea-bird. It breeds in great numbers in the Irish sea at Grassholm and is consequently commonly seen off the coast of Anglesey. Sometimes, when there are schools of small fish offshire, gannets gather in crowds with gulls, terns and porpoises and make a splendid display as they plunge for their fishy prey time and again with enormous gusto and splash. Being very large and very white the gannet is easily seen when far out to sea and identified by its pointed cruciform shape of attenuated wings, sharply pointed tail, long neck and dagger bill.

The plate on page 95 reproduces drawings of a juvenile gannet: so dark and strangely different from the almost wholly white adult, it can, when swimming, be mistaken for a diver or a cormorant. Patchwork birds changing into mature plumage can be even more puzzling. It is interesting that the Australasian gannet which is very similar in most respects – and indeed, seen in flight, seems scarcely to differ, though it does have more black in the wings and some in the tail – has a juvenile plumage that is not wholly dark.

GANNET (*Sula bassana*)

'Gannet. Juvenile ♂ obtained Nov. 5th from Mr Faulkes, who found it in a field near his farm of Bodrwyn. No sign of injury on it. Cause of death unknown. Tail feathers much abraded. Almost ½" of bare quill at tip of two centre feathers. Wing 443 mm. Bill to tail 880 mm. Drawn Nov. 6th–7th '74.'

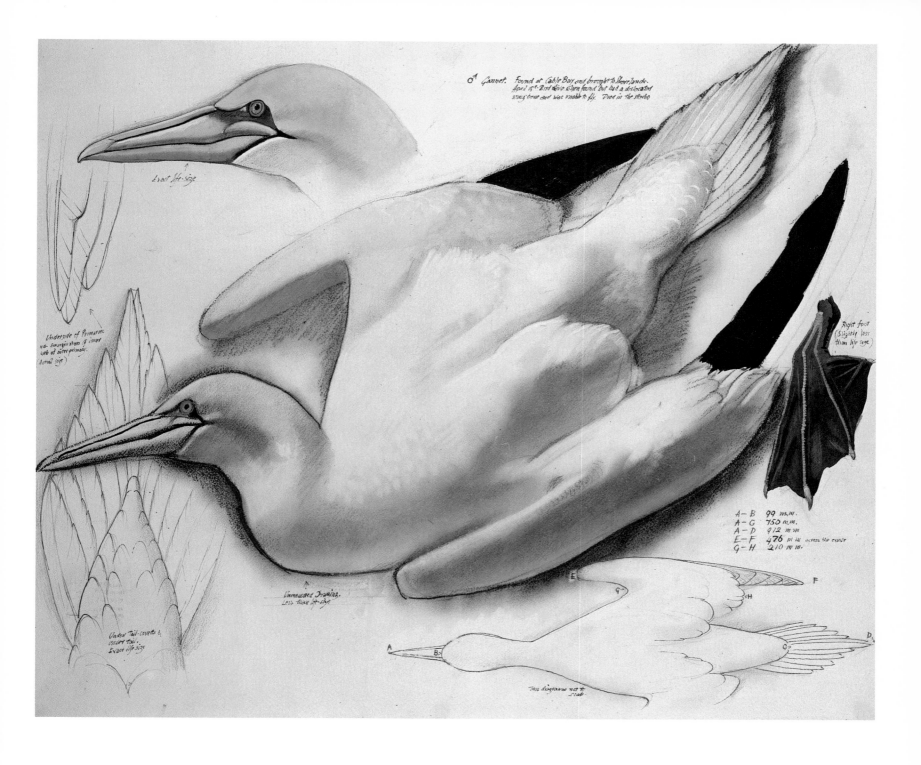

GANNET (*Sula bassana*)
'♂ Gannet. Found at Cable Bay and brought to Shorelands,
April 15th. Bird alive when found but had a dislocated wing-
bone and was unable to fly. Died in the studio. A–B 99 mm.
A–G 750 mm. A–D 912 mm. E–F 476 mm. across the curve.
G–H 210 mm.

POMARINE SKUA

The pomarine skua does not breed at all in Britain and is known only as a somewhat scarce late summer coastal passage bird, much less numerous than the arctic skua which, however, seems never to have come into Tunnicliffe's hands. The subject of Tunnicliffe's drawing is a juvenile bird found dead in October on Aberffraw dunes. It is not easy to distinguish pomarine from arctic skuas in this plumage and evidently Tunnicliffe was puzzled at first by the lack of points on the central tail feathers, supposing it to be a juvenile arctic skua, and only later decided correctly that it was a juvenile pomarine skua.

Skuas, of which there are several species, are all more or less dark brown birds of piratical habits, deriving much of their food by pestering other sea-birds, gulls and especially terns, to give up or even to disgorge their prey. The word *skua* seems to refer to the dark brown colour. In North America it is confined to the great skua or bonxie (*Stercorarius skua*), the smaller, more agile birds, including the pomarine, being called *jaegers*. The word *pomarine*, formerly *pomatorhine*, refers to the lidded nostrils and could apply equally to any of the group but by custom is confined to *Stercorarius pomarinus*.

The adult pomarine skua has the elongated central tail feathers curiously twisted but the twist is not yet developed in Tunnicliffe's specimen. The much more common arctic skua, when adult, has the central tail feathers elongated and sharply pointed.

All the skuas breed in the far north and of the four only the arctic skua and the great skua breed in Britain and these only in the north of Scotland, on the mainland and in the Hebrides and Orkney and Shetland. The pomarine and long-tailed skuas are confined as breeding birds to sub-arctic lands but when the breeding season is over they move southward, mostly, it is believed, over the sea, but a few join the British breeding skuas that work their way to warmer seas and shores in autumn by way of British coasts.

POMARINE SKUA (*Stercorarius pomarinus*)
'Juv. Pomarine Skua. Found Oct. 28th on Aberffraw dunes by Eric and Ruth Cotes-Preedy. (This bird partly plucked on centre of breast). Wing 350 mm. Bill to tail 18". Approx. wing span 44". The two centre tail feathers had no trace of points at their tips but were as rounded as the adjacent pair.'

When wing is extended white on inner webs of outer primaries is more apparent.

Juv. Pomatorhine Skua. Found Oct. 28th on Aberffraw dunes by Eric & Ruth Cotes-Preedy. (This bird partly plucked on centre of breast) Wing – 350 m.m.   Bill-tip   Tail – 18"   Approx wing-span. 44"

The two centre tail feathers had no trace of points at their tips but were as rounded as the adjacent pair.

Wing-tips project beyond tail.

BLACK-HEADED GULL

The plate above includes drawings of two adult black-headed gulls, the main figures being in winter plumage with head and foot of another bird in summer dress. Tunnicliffe made another sheet of drawings (not reproduced) from a live first winter bird which was 'caught at Redesmere with a wing injury on November 10th, brought home and fed on raw meat (and) herring liver. He also ate wood chippings from my boxwood blocks. Released Redesmere December 3rd. Flew off very capably'.

Opposite is a juvenile. The brown areas on the head and body in the first feather are very rapidly lost and the full juvenile plumage is rarely seen far away from the breeding colonies. The first winter plumage is usually assumed by September and often, at least in part, much earlier. The large figures above show the winter plumage of the adult when the dark brown hood of the breeding plumage is almost entirely lost and the deep blood-red of bill and feet becomes progressively lighter and brighter.

BLACK-HEADED GULL (*Larus ridibundus*)
'Black-headed Gull. Brought in alive by Glanfryn Williams. Feb. 5th 1954. It was in a weak and exhausted state. (There had been days and nights of keen frost and there was much ice on the estuary). It died in the studio. Wing 310 mm. Bill to tail 15¼". Span approx. 36".'

Notes on the head and foot at the centre:
'♀ B. H. Gull. July 25th. Found dead on beach. Brought in by village children. Wing 310 mm. Bill to tail 15". Wing identical to that of the winter bird except that the pale tips present on the 4th, 5th and 6th primaries were worn away on this bird. Webs are darker and duller than toes.'

BLACK-HEADED GULL (*Larus ridibundus*)
'♂ Juvenile black-headed gull. Obtained July 14th '65 from Eileen Wheeler. Found Anglesey. Wing 272 mm. Bill to tail 360 mm. approx.'

♂ Juvenile BLACK-HEADED GULL. Obtained July 14ᵗʰ '65 from Aleom Wheeler. Forrest Anglesey. Wing 278 mm. Bill to Tail. 360 mm approx.

Left leg
×1

×1½

RAZORBILL

The drawings of a razorbill (*opposite*) were made from a bird found, oiled and dead, in Anglesey in December. It is accordingly in winter plumage. These birds frequent our rocky coasts during the breeding season but in winter they shed some of the dark colouring and lead a marine life on the continental shelf and in the western Mediterranean. At this time they are liable to be overcome by a long spell of bad weather and corpses are not infrequently washed ashore.

The breeding colonies are located round most of the rocky coasts of Britain except that there are now few along the east and south coasts of England. They are often associated with colonies of guillemots but they do not usually, as guillemots do, breed on open, narrow ledges, but occupy for preference crannies among boulders and similar sites with some sort of overhead shelter, and they are frequently found nest-ing singly or in small groups quite independently.

James Fisher might well have said that the razorbill and guillemot are the nearest things to penguins that swim in the North Atlantic. It was not always so. Until about the middle of the last century these northern waters were inhabited by the great auk or garefowl which was also known as the penguin (Willughby says it is 'called Penguin by our Seamen') and it was only after discovery of the penguins of the southern oceans that the word was transferred to this group. The razorbill indeed gives a very good idea of what the extinct great auk must have looked like for, apart from the much greater size of the garefowl, its relatively much shorter wings, and a white patch about the eyes, it was surely of very similar appearance. Like penguins it swam expertly on and under the water and on land it stood erect. It could not fly.

RAZORBILL *(Alca torda)*
'♀ Razorbill. Obtained Dec. 10th '69 from Kenneth Williams
at Trearddur Bay. This bird found dead and oiled. Wing
197 mm. Bill to tail 400 mm. approx.'

GUILLEMOT

These drawings of a guillemot (*opposite*) were made from an oiled bird found by Ronald Lockley at Aberdaron in October. Lockley cleaned it and fed it on sardines but it died on its way to Malltraeth. It is in winter plumage, as were the birds of two other sheets of drawings that are not reproduced. Tunnicliffe had no measured drawing of the breeding plumage but there are many studies in his sketchbooks made at the breeding colonies at South Stack and elsewhere. He notes that this bird was 'very dark on its upper parts with barely a trace of brown on head or neck' and suggests that it was probably of the northern race of guillemot. The dark chocolate brown of head and neck is more noticeable in the breeding plumage than in winter, even in the southern form. In winter the guillemot lives entirely on the sea though not usually, unlike its relative Brünnich's guillemot, far beyond the continental shelf. It is frequently a storm casualty and is washed up dead or moribund on the winter beaches of Britain.

Guillemots breed in large and crowded colonies usually on narrow ledges on vertical cliff faces. They build no nest and lay but a single large egg of very various colour on the bare rock. The ledge is often so narrow and crowded that, save for the almost conical shape of the egg, they must surely all be lost into the sea. The egg is so designed that it revolves when pushed rather than rolls. Although silent in winter, guillemots at their breeding colonies utter a constant loud murmuring or growling sound that, combined with the vociferous chorus of 'kitty waak' from the kittiwakes that often breed on the same, or nearby, cliffs, makes a swelling avian din that has to be heard to be believed.

The guillemot in North America is known as the *murre* and this is a now obsolete or local word for the bird in Britain, although it seems to have been applied equally, or even more frequently, to the razorbill. Both Bewick (1804) and Willughby (1678) give murre as an alternative name for the razorbill but not for the guillemot. However it seems clearly to refer to the murmuration from the breeding colony and as such is more appropriately assigned to the louder and more crowded guillemot. The word *guillemot* is variously supposed to be derived from two words for gull or to be a word of the same kind as magpie (Maggie the pie) and jackdaw (Jack the daw) in which a familiar bird is given, as it were, a Christian name. Willughby says the bird is 'called by the Welsh and Manksmen a Guillem'.

GUILLEMOT *(Uria aalge)*

'Guillemot. Drawn Oct. 5th '54. Obtained by Ronald
Lockley on Aberdaron beach. The bird was oiled on the left
side, tail and wing tips. Lockley, Norris and [unidentified]
partially cleaned it and fed it on sardines and on Oct. 3rd
brought it by car from Aberdaron to Malltraeth. They kindly
offered to let me keep the bird but on opening the box found
the bird quite dead. (All drawings actual size.) This bird
very dark on its upper parts with barely a trace of brown on
head or neck. Streaks on flanks blue-black. Probably
Northern Guillemot.'

LITTLE AUK

The little auk is an arctic bird. It breeds in Greenland, Jan Mayen, Grimsey, Bear Island, Spitzbergen, Novaya Zemlya and Franz Josef Land, nowhere south of the Arctic Circle. The breeding colonies are said to be enormously populous. No nest is made. The egg is laid on the bare ground in a cranny among rocks. The birds feed almost exclusively on plankton. Outside the breeding season they are entirely marine and are found usually not far from the pack ice. They do however tend to move southward in winter. They gather perhaps in greatest numbers in the waters east and south of Newfoundland, according to Wynne-Edwards their 'winter metropolis', but they visit British waters irregularly and sometimes appear here in very large numbers. Prolonged gales occasionally drive them ashore and then they may be found, dead or dying, inland, as Tunnicliffe's subject was. Wynne-Edwards says that the little auk 'must be one of the most numerous and successful of all birds. Few so little are so free from predatory enemies: and possibly that is why, like lemmings, dovekies periodically seek their own destruction on such a grand scale'. For in North America little auks are officially called, more attractively, *dovekies*. The name is hardly used in England but Montagu does give 'Greenland dove' as an alternative to little auk.

LITTLE AUK *(Plautus alle)*
'♀ Little Auk. Found alive on (Tyn Lon) the old road from Llangefni to Holyhead on Jan. 22nd '49 and sent dead to T. G. Walker who brought it to me Jan. 27th. All drawings life size except where stated otherwise. Wing 125 mm. Beak to tail 207 mm. 12 tail feathers all black excepting the two outer which have white spot at tips.'

12 TAIL FEATHERS
ALL BLACK EXCEPTING
THE 2 OUTER WHICH
HAVE WHITE SPOT AT
TIPS

× 2

× 2.

× 2,
LEFT
FOOT.

♀ **LITTLE AUK.** Found alive on (TYN LON)
the old road from Llangefni to
Holyhead on Jan 22ⁿᵈ '49 and
sent to T.G. WALKER who brought
it to me. Drown Jan 27ᵗʰ
All drawings life size except where
stated otherwise.

WING — 125 mm.
BEAK TO TAIL. 207 mm

LITTLE TERN

Considering the popularity of terns as subjects for Tunnicliffe's pictures and the number and variety of terns in summer in south-west Anglesey it is surprising there are so few represented in his collection of measured drawings. Besides this sheet of drawings of a little tern there are two sheets (not reproduced here) made from a common tern from the Ribble, and no other. But the sketchbooks have many drawings of terns.

All terns breed on sandy shores on spits, on shingle banks and in dunes. In consequence they are all subjected to more or less harassment by increasing summer disturbance of sand beaches by man who encroaches more and more on formerly lonely and unfrequented shores. The other British terns breed in relatively compact and usually large colonies which can be protected, if the will be there, but the little tern favours small and scattered colonies or even solitary nest-sites, and effective protection is very difficult. Nests may be inadvertently destroyed by the most well-meaning beach stroller. Thus the little tern has become in recent years, after the always very scarce roseate tern, the rarest of terns and very much an endangered species.

Like other sea terns or sea swallows the little tern is a summer visitor to Britain. It is, as its name implies, markedly smaller than the common, arctic, roseate and Sandwich terns and it usually fishes closer inshore in tidal channels and pools where it may be watched hovering with rapidly beating wings before plunging vertically into the water to catch, usually, a sand-eel or a sprat. The Cob pool at Malltraeth and the pools and channels on the estuary are favourite fishing grounds, as are the waters round Llanddwyn Island.

LITTLE TERN (*Sterna albifrons*)
'Little Tern. Obtained from D. Morgan June 24th who found it dead beside its nest at Abermenai. Wing 178 mm. Span 19″ approx. Bill to tail 9⅜″.'

Little Tern. Obtained from D. Morgan
June 24ᵗʰ who found it dead beside
its nest at Aber Menai.
Wing 178 mm. Span. 19" Approx.
Bill to Tail - 9⅗"

Right foot

× 2

WOODCOCK

The drawings opposite were made from a woodcock purchased in Macclesfield. Tunnicliffe has worked with painstaking care to record exactly the intricate pattern of the feathers which is so very effective in making the bird nearly invisible when it is crouching among the brown and gold of dead leaves. The woodcock breeds in suitable territory, mostly woodland, over much of Britain, but it is nocturnal in habit and this, taken together with its most effective protective colouration, results in the bird being little known. Its display flights about the breeding territory, known as 'roding', are conspicuous enough, but occur only at dawn and dusk. Great numbers of woodcock enter Britain from the Continent in October and November, accompanied frequently on the same easterly breeze by the *woodcock owl* (the short-eared owl) and the *woodcock's mate*, the tiny goldcrest which at one time was supposed only to be able to cross the North Sea by riding on the woodcock's back. Strangely, it can and does cross, in large numbers, although at times in a brisk wind it seems to do little more than sustain itself in the air, drifting like a butterfly exhausted to the shore.

When the woodcock arrive they are suddenly everywhere and may be put up, several in a short walk, from the rusty bracken and fallen leaves of heath and woodland. They will alight only a little further on but are rarely found a second time. Only in hard weather will they be seen feeding in the open in daylight when they wander through meadows and over lawns, probing for softer places in the frost-hardened ground. At such times they may be encountered two or three or more together but they are normally solitary birds.

WOODCOCK (*Scolopax rusticola*)
'Woodcock, purchased in Macclesfield on Oct. 15th '40.'

CURLEW

The curlew (*opposite*) is one of those many birds that Tunnicliffe obtained by purchase from a poulterer's shop in the Shambles, Manchester. In order to display this large bird fully, Tunnicliffe worked on two sheets of paper. Only one of these is reproduced here. The other sheet has drawings of the upper and under surfaces of the spread wing.

The curlew is a common bird of moorland up to about 2,000 ft. where it makes its presence known in spring by its wonderful musical song. In recent times it has begun to breed at lower levels and is now probably more numerous on rough low ground, heathland and damp pasture than it is in high moorland. Outside the breeding season it gathers into flocks, some of them very large, and is often to be seen in cliff-top pastures and arable land round the coast of Wales. It also feeds on the shore and Tunnicliffe made several exhibition pictures of resting and feeding flocks in such localities.

The curlew is known as the *whaup* in Scotland, a word which, like *curlew*, is realistically derived from one of the musical calls of the bird.

In America the long-billed curlew (*Numenius americana*) has an even more phenomenally long and down-curved bill than has the European curlew. It is also a larger bird, more rufous, and lacking the pale rump of *N. arquata*. The eastern race of *N. arquata* is often accorded specific rank as *N. Madagascariensis* but is little different from *arquata* except in lacking a pale rump. It is a trans-equatorial migrant and appears in the southern summer on Australian and New Zealand shores in small numbers from its breeding home in East Siberia.

CURLEW *(Numenius arquata)*
'Curlew ♀. Purchased in the Shambles, Manchester, Jan.
17th. Informed it came from Ireland. Exact life size.'

BAR-TAILED GODWIT

The bar-tailed godwit is not a British nesting bird but it is a common passage migrant and winter visitor from its breeding grounds in the Arctic and sub-Arctic. It is essentially a coastal bird and, with the sanderling, is probably the principal denizen of the tide-edge. It is not often seen far inland. Tunnicliffe's bird came from Wagstaffe in February and thus is in winter plumage. In the breeding season it assumes a rich red feather on head, neck and underparts which is not often seen in full in Britain although flocks passing northward in spring will frequently have a sprinkling of birds with at least a patchy display of the summer finery.

Although European birds do not go much further south than west Africa, and indeed many stay the winter in Britain, the eastern race of the bar-tailed godwit is a regular trans-equatorial migrant and great flocks are found on Australian estuaries in the southern summer. On the several harbours in the neighbourhood of Auckland there must be many thousands of these birds and they make a fine spectacle resting at high tide in the bright sunshine on the glittering white shell-banks of say the Firth of Thames. Before they leave for the far north in April most of them will have assumed red plumage in preparation for the breeding season. The eastern bird lacks the whitish rump of the European race and is larger, but not noticeably so in the field. The female of both races has a longer bill than does the male.

The black-tailed godwit is a related species that appears at Malltraeth in April and May, though it does not stay to breed. It reappears in July and August. The spring birds are usually in the fine red breeding plumage and recur frequently in Tunnicliffe's sketchbooks (*A Sketchbook of Birds*, plates 47 and 58; *Sketches of Bird Life*, plates 79 and 104). Unfortunately he seems never to have had a specimen of a black-tailed godwit from which to make a measured drawing. Superficially similar, on the ground, to a bar-tailed godwit, the black-tailed godwit is immediately quite distinct in flight owing to the bold black and white pattern of its wings and tail.

BAR-TAILED GODWIT *(Limosa lapponica)*
'Bar-tailed Godwit. Adult winter, sent to R. Wagstaffe in
Feb. 1939.'

WHIMBREL

The whimbrel (*opposite*) was shot at Malltraeth in September. It is a bird which breeds in Britain only in the far north of Scotland and commonly so only in Shetland. It is known in the rest of Britain as a common passage migrant both in spring and in autumn, principally along the coasts. It is very similar to the curlew but is smaller and has a shorter and less vigorously decurved bill. The boldly striped crown is a characteristic feature as is the sevenfold stuttering, rippling cry, so different from the curlew's shorter 'coor-lee' and 'whaup'. It may be supposed that this cry is the origin of the word whimbrel, *el* being a diminutive and the first syllable, according to Potter and Sargent, being a corruption of *whimmer*, related to *whimper*.

The American race of the whimbrel, formerly known as the Hudsonian curlew, differs from the European race in having almost uniform upperparts. The European race, as of the curlew, has a whitish rump. The Asiatic race is very similar to the European race. Both American and Asiatic whimbrels are trans-equatorial migrants and appear on Australian and New Zealand shores in the northern winter. There they may be distinguished by the presence or absence of the pale rump.

WHIMBREL (*Numenius phaeopus*)
'Whimbrel. Shot Sept. 1st. Malltraeth by Mr Whitaker. Drawn Sept. 4th & 5th. 1950. Wing 236 mm. Span about 28". Length, bill to tail, 16¼". Bill (straight measurement from forehead feathers to tip) 74 mm. Weight 15 oz.'

WHIMBREL. SHOT SEPT. 1st MALLTRAETH
BY Mr WHITAKER. DRAWN SEPT 4th & 5th 1950
— WING 236 mm. SPAN. ABOUT 28"
LENGTH, BILL TO TAIL, 16 1/4"
BILL (straight measurement from forehead feathers
to tip) 74 m.m.
Weight 15 ozs.

SCAPULAR AT A.   AT B.

long Inner Secondaries of
Right Wing.

longest Inner Secondary at C.   LEFT LEG.

DUNLIN

The dunlin is without doubt the most common of the small waders that frequent British coasts and marshes at all seasons. It breeds in Britain on northern wet moorlands in the same sort of country as does the golden plover. Indeed it is sometimes known as the 'plover's page', probably because it frequently follows a circling plover in seeking to discomfit an intruder. In the breeding plumage shown in the bottom right hand birds, obtained from a breeding ground on Axe Edge, near Buxton, the dunlin has a warm chestnut back and a black patch on the belly. Indeed it is, or was formerly, known in North America as the red-backed sandpiper. But in winter (*left hand figures*) the dunlin is a notably dun bird; hence, no doubt, the name. This one was bought in the Shambles. The top right bird was shot at Malltraeth and is a juvenile. Dunlins vary greatly, not only in plumage but also in size and in length and decurvature of bill. Consequently, notwithstanding that they have a characteristic hunched attitude and typical feeding mannerisms, they are often surmised, incorrectly, to be other, rarer species by over-eager bird watchers.

DUNLIN (*Calidris alpina*)

Left hand figures:
'Dunlin ♂ Sexed R. Wagstaffe. Purchased in Shambles, Manchester, Feb. 24th. '39. All drawings measured exact life size except where stated otherwise.'

Top right figures:
'♂ Juv. Dunlin. Obtained Malltraeth Bay, Oct. 18th. '66 by M. E. D. Wing 120.5 mm. Bill to tail 213 mm.

Lower right figures (A):
'♂ Dunlin. Found Axe Edge, Derbyshire, mid-May by D. M. This bird still moulting. Many old and abraded feathers among new summer plumage. Wing 109 mm. Bill to tail 173 mm.

Lower right figures (B):
'♀ Dunlin. May 26th. Axe Edge, Derbyshire. Similar in plumage to the ♂ above in its moulting and abraded feathers. Wing 115 mm. Bill to tail 172 mm. approx.

GOLDEN PLOVER

The two golden plovers (*opposite*) were both obtained from Axe Edge in Derbyshire in June. The upper bird is a male, the lower, with less black on the underparts, a female. Golden plovers which breed further north than Britain have an even more distinguished breeding plumage with solid black on face, fore-neck and underparts, bordered by a broad white band. Birds in this fine plumage can sometimes be seen on passage in spring in Anglesey and Tunnicliffe was always excited by their appearance. *Shorelands Summer Diary* has a painting of them (page 28). The black underparts of all races is lost in winter when the birds feed in flocks in the fields and salt-marshes often with lapwings. Then they can easily be overlooked, their gold and brown plumage merging readily with the sere winter vegetation.

The closely related grey plover does not breed in Britain but is a common passage migrant and winter visitor. There is no measured drawing but the bird appears from time to time in Tunnicliffe's sketchbooks (see *A Sketchbook of Birds*, plate 32). It is very similar to the golden plover but it is less apt to be seen in large flocks and has a different habitat, preferring shore mud to the grassy pastures favoured by the golden plover. Rather larger than the golden plover it lacks the golden yellow of that bird (though immature grey plovers can be deceptively buff) and is at once distinguished by voice and, in flight, by the black splash on the underwing. It is a most beautiful bird in breeding plumage when its underparts are a solid black separated by a band of pure white from the spangled silver-grey of the upper parts.

GOLDEN PLOVER (*Pluvialis apricaria*)
'♂ Golden Plover from Axe Edge, Derbyshire, June 10th '67.
Wing 182 mm. Bill to tail 273 mm. Long inner secondaries
missing, as also were some upper tail coverts.'

Lower right figures:
'♀ Golden Plover from Axe Edge, Derbyshire, June 10th.
Wing 190 mm. Bill to tail 275 mm. In both male and female
the mandibles made contact only at the tip and at the gape.'

REDSHANK

This redshank (*opposite*) was shot at Malltraeth in November. The redshank is a common breeding wader in Britain on almost any wet ground, particularly in the north. It is a conspicious and well-known species from its bright red legs and the broad white crescent along the rear edge of the spread wing but perhaps more on account of its loud, melodious whistle as it noisily flies around whenever disturbed, particularly on its nesting ground. Indeed it is known to many as the 'warden of the marshes' and is regarded as a nuisance by wild-fowlers because its noisy watchfulness alerts other birds not of themselves so readily disturbed.

The dusky, or spotted redshank is not illustrated. Apparently no specimen came into Tunnicliffe's hands although it is commonly to be seen at migration times on the Cob pool and he made numerous sketches of it. It is a larger bird than the redshank and its wings are uniformly dark above. It does not breed in Britain.

REDSHANK *(Tringa totanus)*
'Redshank (Probably adult) found by Winifred on the road
by Malltraeth Lake. There was a shot wound in the breast.
Nov. 6th '53. Length, bill to tail, neck extended, 11½". Wing
across curve 163 mm.'

MISCELLANEOUS BIRDS

CHOUGH

The curt note on this sheet (*opposite*) is in Winifred's writing and it is possible that the drawing, wholly or in part, was done by her when Charles was busy and under pressure.

The chough is a diminishing species of coastal cliffs and some mountains in Wales, Ireland and some of the Hebrides. It used sometimes to be called the Cornish chough but occurs in Cornwall no longer. The choughs of Lleyn occasionally visit south-west Anglesey in winter and Tunnicliffe's bird, caught in a rabbit trap at Pen-y-Sarn in February, was no doubt one such. They are perhaps best seen in Britain in Pembrokeshire where they are a common sight on the cliff tops, probing for ants with their curved scarlet bills into thrift tussocks and similar vegetation, or circling and calling 'chough' along the cliff face and over the sea. They are however still more numerous on the west and south coasts of Ireland. In Britain and Ireland they are only very occasionally found away from coastal cliffs but in the Alps, in Iberia and in North Africa they occur principally on inland cliffs in mountainous regions.

The chough that cheekily frequents cafés, restaurants and mountain-railway stations high in the Alps, even above the snow-line, is not the chough of British and Irish cliffs (*Pyrrhocorax pyrrhocorax*) but a related and very similar species, the alpine chough (*Pyrrhocorax graculus*). This is also an all black bird with red legs but the bill of *graculus* is yellow, not red, and much shorter than that of *pyrrhocorax*. *Pyrrhocorax* does occur in the Alps but is usually shy of man.

Bill × 2

Tip of a secondary.

Tip of tail feather
4 B from outside on right.

From Wack
Rabbit Trap Nebo Penysarn
18/2/48

CHOUGH (*Pyrrhocorax pyrrhocorax*)
'From Wack. Rabbit trap. Nebo, Penysarn. 18.2.48.'

RAVEN

The raven is the largest of the crow family and nowadays is a bird mostly of cliffs and mountain tops. A pair used to nest on the ridge of rock that runs through Newborough Warren to Llanddwyn. Tunnicliffe's specimen was shot on the Warren. There is little doubt that the raven was at one time common over much of England but persecution by man has driven it effectively into rocky and mountainous areas and to sea-cliffs. Virtually unknown now in the lowlands of England it is still common in the West Country, in Wales and in the Lake District and the mountainous areas of Scotland. On the popular, well-tramped mountains of North Wales and the Lake District, once having left the buzzards and crows with the last of the trees, one will often see no bird but the odd meadow pipit until reaching the top and then, circling, tumbling and croaking over the crags of the summit, there will be ravens to remind one that the hills are not, yet, just a gymnasium for stretching human legs.

A much larger bird than the crow, the raven has a different call, a short croak not at all like the *caw* of the crow, and its silhouette in the air is different with a longer, more rounded tail. The loose feathers of the throat give it a markedly bearded appearance and the bill is heavy with the culmen strongly curved. These features are well shown in Tunnicliffe's drawing where also the shine and gloss and iridescent colour of the black plumage is marvellously rendered.

Within the illustration, handwritten notes read:

RAVEN. Obtained Newborough Warren.
Oct 1ˢᵗ '58. (M. Davenport.)
Length (flat) Bill to Tail 25"
W. Span approx. 50". (All drawings
Wing. 415 mm. 1/1 size)

RAVEN (*Corvus corax*)
'Raven. Obtained Newborough Warren. Octo. 1st'58. (M.
Davenport). Length (flat) Bill to tail 25". W. Span approx.
50". Wing 415 mm. All drawings life size.'

HOODED CROW

At one time regarded as a species distinct from the black carrion crow the grey and black hooded crow is now considered to be a race of the same species, *Corvus corone*. Where the ranges of the two forms overlap there is interbreeding giving rise to an intermediate zone of varying width inhabited in part by hybrids. In England the crows of summer are all carrion crows as also they are in southern Scotland, but as one goes north in Scotland hooded crows appear on a line roughly from Glasgow to Aberdeen. The crows of Ireland and the Isle of Man are nearly all hooded crows. Tunnicliffe's specimen came from Inverness and his drawings extended onto two sheets, one only of which is reproduced. He also made a sheet of drawings (not reproduced) of a carrion crow from East Cheshire.

A similar situation obtains in continental Europe where the breeding crow of France, Iberia, Denmark and West Germany is the carrion crow but east of, roughly, the Elbe and south of the Alps, from Scandinavia south to Italy and the Balkans and eastward across Russia to the Yenesei the crows are hooded. Eastward from the Yenesei farther into Siberia and the crows become black again. It is supposed that the last ice age separated crows into unconnected populations which were separate long enough to develop differences only in plumage but that their ranges again expanded after the retreat of the ice and the two groups re-joined before differences were sufficiently far-reaching to inhibit interbreeding.

The crows of the north and east of Europe migrate south and west in autumn and in some winters large numbers of crows of hooded plumage arrive in eastern England and spread over the country, returning to their breeding territories in Scandinavia and the Baltic countries with the arrival of spring.

♂ Hooded Crow from Inverness, mid January, 1969.

WING. 320 mm, BILL TO TAIL. 484 mm, WING-SPAN. 837 mm (33")

HOODED CROW (*Corvus corone*)
'♂ Hooded Crow from Inverness, mid January 1969. Wing
320 mm. Bill to tail 484 mm. Wing span 837 mm. (33").'

JAY

The handsome jay is a bird primarily of woodland and, like the magpie, is much persecuted by gamekeepers. The specimen from which the drawings opposite were made came from the wood at Bodorgan. It favours particularly oakwoods and acorns are a principal winter food. It buries them in autumn and disinters them later. Those overlooked no doubt contribute to the spread of oakwoods. It is a noisy bird at most seasons, uttering its linen-tearing, rasping cry when disturbed, but when nesting it can be remarkably silent and unobtrusive. Although it dwells very largely in woodland, and in the breeding season almost exclusively so, it will furtively raid the surrounding country for garden peas and for the eggs and young of garden birds. With the decline in the number of gamekeepers it has increased markedly in this century and, like the magpie, has found city suburbs to its liking and dwells successfully in parks and bosky gardens. In such localities it may occasionally come to bird tables but it is less a scavenger on human affairs than the bold and flashy magpie and far less conspicuous.

Within the illustration (handwritten field notes):

♀ Jay. Obtained June 18ᵗʰ 65.
from David Cunliffe, Trefeilir.
Bodorgan.
Wing 184 mm (Ends of flights worn
or damaged) Bill to Tail. 350 mm.

Inner Secondaries
these feather details
from right wing.

longest
Primary
Covert

from Bastard
Wing

Secondary
Covert

Right foot.

JAY (*Garrulus glandarius*)
'♀ Jay. Obtained June 18th'65 from David Cunliffe, Trefeilir,
Bodorgan. Wing 184 mm. (Ends of flights worn or
damaged). Bill to tail 350 mm.'

CUCKOO

The cuckoo is a famous bird on two accounts. The spring song of the male is known to everyone though many who are familiar with the 'wandering voice' will not know its author and few indeed are familiar with the bubbling cry of the female. Its second claim to fame stems from its, in human terms, unsavoury habit of laying its eggs in the nests of small birds, particularly of meadow pipits and dunnocks, and taking no further interest in their nurture. Hence the word 'cuckold' for the deceived husband whose wife foists on him another man's child. The young cuckoo is even more reprehensible in human terms, for, once hatched, it immediately evicts the foster-parent's eggs or young. The cuckoo is often said to look like a sparrowhawk when on the wing but it has more pointed wings and, when spread, a graduated tail with white tips, as Tunnicliffe's drawings show.

The word *cuckoo* is, of course, onomatopoeic. There is an older word for the bird, *gowk*, which is still prevalent in Scotland.

Cuckoos are summer visitors and are widespread and common in their season over the British Isles though they are said in recent years to have diminished in eastern England. Certainly here in Norfolk, in the north of the county, it has seemed to be but a passage bird in some recent years, singing only for a week or so in later April and early May. But perhaps there has been some recovery, for in 1981 and 1982 cuckoo song has again been continuous until the end of June. It is a caterpillar-eater and its food may have become more scarce as a result of the use of pesticides in agriculture.

There are many cuckoos the world over and they are by no means all given, as is *Cuculus canorus*, to foisting their family affairs on other species. The cuckoos that visit New Zealand from the north in summer, the shining cuckoo and the long-tailed cuckoo, are parasitic, respectively and principally, on the grey warbler and the whitehead, but the common cuckoos of North America, the black-billed and yellow-billed cuckoos, build their own nests. The familiar brood parasite there is a bird of a quite different family, the cowbird.

Brood parasitic birds are not invariably successful. In Britain the cuckoo's egg when deposited in, for example, a blackcap's or a spotted flycatcher's nest is usually evicted. Also in America the cowbird's egg is usually destroyed when laid in the nest of an American robin or of a catbird.

CUCKOO (*Cuculus canorus*)
'♂ Cuckoo. Found dead by children. Malltraeth May 14th.
Wing 225 mm. Bill to tail 14″ (355 mm.) Span approx. 23″.
Edges of tail feathers abraded and most of the white spots
were missing from the margins.'

NIGHTJAR

The nightjar is a strange bird. It has much in common with the woodcock though the two birds are not at all related. It is nocturnal, breeds on the ground among dead leaves where the brown, grey and golden delicately patterned feathers provide a perfect protective colouring. Both birds are, as near as maybe, invisible as they sit motionless among the brown and gold leaves of heath or woodland floor. Tunnicliffe's meticulous drawings well display the marvellously intricate and beautifully decorative plumage. The bird is probably best known from its curious song, described by B. W. Tucker as a 'sustained, vibrant, churring trill, like an excessively rapid but somewhat *wooden* or slightly muffled tapping, not at all sharp or metallic'. This churring song used to be a common sound of a summer night on almost any suitable sandy heath or sparse woodland but the nightjar has now become an uncommon bird in Britain except perhaps for the counties along the south coast where there is more country to its liking. It is a summer visitor and does not usually arrive until early May. It feeds on insects, particularly on the beetles and moths that fly by night. With long wings and tail it is agile and graceful in flight and the capture of its prey is aided by an unusually wide gape fringed with bristles and, no doubt, also by its exceptionally large eyes and ear apertures.

A former, and still locally used name for the nightjar is *goatsucker*. It must be supposed that this misnomer arose when goatherds, seeing the bird flying at dusk round and about the sleeping goats, jumped to the wrong conclusion. The same false accusation is contained in the scientific name for the genus, *Caprimulgus*. Doubtless nightjars so engaged are in pursuit of the insects that gather round animals.

The structure of the very small feet of nightjars is unusual. The hind toe points inward and the short outer toes are connected by a membrane to the long middle toe as far as the middle joint. The claw of the middle toe has comb-like serrations as in the heron. The bird rarely walks when on the ground and when perching it usually lies along the branch rather than crossways.

In southern Europe and North Africa there are two other nightjars, the red-necked nightjar and the Egyptian nightjar, both of which have been recorded occasionally in Britain. In Africa south of the Sahara there are many species of this essentially tropical group.

NIGHTJAR (*Caprimulgus europaeus*)
'♀ Nightjar. Sent by Ednyfed Davies M.P. who found it on the road between Abergavenny and Pontypool. May 24th '66. Tail badly damaged with a number of tail feathers missing. Wing 186 mm.'

Right leg & foot
x

Middle claw
x

xO Nightjar. Sent by Llanfyllin Davies M.P.
who found it on the road between Abergavenny & Bwlypost.
May 24ᵗʰ '66. Tail badly damaged with a number of tail
feathers missing. Wing 186 mm.

x

TURTLE DOVE

The turtle dove is a summer visitor to Britain where it is common in the south and east of England but scarce in the north, almost absent from Scotland and rare in the western parts of Wales. Tunnicliffe's specimen came from south Lancashire. It is a very beautiful small dove with a soft and sleepy 'coo' that is a delightfully restful characteristic sound of early summer where the bird occurs. Its principal, but by no means exclusive, diet consists of the seeds of fumitory and its summer distribution is said, more or less, to coincide with the distribution of this plant.

If we are to accept the Biblical 'the voice of the turtle is heard in the land' it would appear that in earlier times the word *dove* was not appended. The word *turtle*, in this context, is doubtless derived from the Latin *turtur* and is onomatopoeic. The reptile of the same name probably acquired it in a quite different way, as a corruption of the Spanish *tortuga*. Possibly familiarity with these animals required the distinction of the added *dove*.

The turtle dove is not a city bird, nor is it a hill bird, but a shy rural bird of farmland and fertile countryside. The rather similar collared dove, which in the last century has spread westward across Europe and become a familiar bird everywhere, is, on the other hand, an associate of man and is found in towns and villages but may be scarce in the intervening countryside, except where poultry-keeping or other source of grain may attract it. There must now be few villages where its monotonous 'cuck-oo-cuck', so much less pleasing than the voice of the turtle, is not tiresomely heard.

TURTLE DOVE (*Streptopelia turtur*)
'Turtle Dove ♀. (Half developed eggs found when opened). Obtained June 12th Sth. Lancashire. C. Schofield. Tips of tail feathers much worn. Reconstructed in drawing. Drawn June 14th. All drawings measured. Many new quills found growing when plucked, especially on breast. Crop full of wheat.'

Turtle-dove. ♀ (half developed eggs found when opened)
Obtained June 12th. Sth Lancashire. C. Scholfield.
Tips of tail-feathers much worn. Reconstructed in
the Drawing.   Drawn June 14th. All drawings naturalsized.
Many new quills found growing when plucked, especially on breast.
Crop full of wheat.

GREEN WOODPECKER

The green woodpecker is the largest of the three British woodpeckers. Tunnicliffe's bird is a female. The male has a crimson moustache. Although this woodpecker is surprisingly common in relatively treeless Anglesey this specimen came from Herefordshire. A juvenile that Tunnicliffe also drew (not reproduced) was found dead at Bodorgan. The bird is in fact by no means exclusively a bird of trees. Much of its diet consists of ants and it feeds to a large extent on the ground. It is a well-known bird on account of its cry, like a loud ringing laugh, which has earned it the other popular name of *yaffle*.

All three woodpeckers in Britain seem to be southern birds. The lesser spotted woodpecker is virtually absent from Scotland and the green woodpecker appeared there only about 1950. The great spotted woodpecker is now widespread in Scotland but was absent from that country for much of the last century. None of the woodpeckers is found in Ireland.

The spotted woodpeckers are pied birds with crimson decoration. They are hardly *spotted* and it would seem better to re-name the larger one the pied woodpecker and the smaller the barred woodpecker. All the British woodpeckers have special adaptations for life as bark-feeders, with two toes fore and two aft, all equipped with large and strong claws, rigidly feathered tails to act as props, a hatchet bill to chip away at bark and rotten wood for insects, and an extraordinarily long and slender tongue capable of great extension and barbed at the end. The green woodpecker may be heard tapping loudly in search for food or in hacking out its nest-hole but it does not usually, as the spotted woodpeckers regularly do, indulge in *drumming*, a form of nuptial 'song' in which the bill is hammered very rapidly against a suitably resounding branch. The sound in the distance is like some elephantine snore.

The green woodpecker climbs upwards on a tree trunk or branch as do the spotted woodpeckers, when it needs to descend it usually proceeds backwards. Another bark feeder, the nuthatch, by contrast, seems to prefer to feed downwards, and usually proceeds head first.

GREEN WOODPECKER (*Picus viridis*)

'Green woodpecker ♀. Obtained from A. V. Cuerden, of Queen Elizabeth's Grammar School, Bromyard, Hereford. Feb. 7th 1954. Wing 166 mm. Bill to tail 13". Outer long tail feather on the right side just showing below the short outer tail feather. (This bird a victim of the cold spell at the beginning of February. It was possible to pull the tongue out until it was quite 4" beyond the tip.'

Top right figure:
'♀ Green woodpecker. Obtained Malltraeth June 8th '64. Probably in first summer plumage because of the spotting on the flanks and undersides. Wing 163 mm. Bill to tail 12¼".'

RING OUZEL

The ring ouzel is a bird of mountain and moorland where it will usually be found in a steep-sided clough or gully, often with water, and usually with an overhanging rowan or crag as a song post. It is a summer visitor to Britain and appears to have diminished in numbers in the last century although it is difficult to see why this should be so since its favoured territory must be little changed. On migration it may be encountered almost anywhere but is rarely noticed. It is perhaps most usually seen in autumn in association with other thrushes at berried trees or bushes. It is very like the blackbird and must often be passed over as such. The characteristic white patch on the breast is obvious only when the bird is facing the observer and is obscure in the female and absent in young birds.

The word *ouzel* is found also in an alternative name for the dipper, namely *water ouzel*, and was applied long ago to the blackbird for which Bewick gives the alternative name *black ouzel*. The German word for *blackbird* is the obviously related *amsel* and this word is given as a provincial alternative by Montagu.

RING OUZEL (*Turdus torquatus*)
Left hand figures:
'♂ Ring Ouzel. Obtained 19th May '65, from Cut-Thorn Hill,
East Cheshire, by M.E.D. Wing 143 mm. Bill to tail 270 mm.

Centre figures:
'♀ Ring Ouzel. Obtained 19th May '65, from Cut-Thorn Hill,
East Cheshire, by M.E.D. Wing 135 mm. Bill to tail, 258 mm.
The feathers of the female, except for a few new ones, were
very worn and abraded, especially those of the flights and
tail. The male was in better condition and although his
wings and tail were rather shabby he had many immaculate
new feathers.'

Right hand figures:
'Juv. ♂ Ring Ouzel. Obtained at Three Shires Head, June
6th or 7th. This bird with down still on the head and not all
tail feathers showing – not long out of the nest.'

DIPPER

The dipper that Tunnicliffe used for these drawings (*opposite*) came from East Cheshire where the bird is common, as indeed it is in the neighbouring Derbyshire. It is a bird of mountain streams, like the grey wagtail, and the two are often seen on the same stretch of river. In the southern Pennines it is common on both limestone and gritstone rivers but it is found in greater or less density in all the hill country of Britain. It is usually seen standing on a stone in mid-river or flying up or down stream on short whirring wings in a bee-line, kingfisher-like, but lacking the vivid, shining hue. If carefully stalked it may be watched about its business for it is not excessively shy. It works the bottom of its favourite clear and rapid waters, dipping first, then wading in deeper until it disappears under the surface, still walking on the bottom. In deeper water it may plop in from a stone or swim and then dive from the surface. One rarely sees more than two birds together, even outside the breeding season, and they seem to have their own length of river and if driven beyond its limits they double back. When resting, the dipper appears as a portly, wren-like figure, with cocked tail, bobbing at intervals and flicking the white nictitating membrane across its eye. It is usually silent except in flight when it utters a repeated clinking note. The warbling song in springtime is very reminiscent of the wren but lacks the astonishing volume of sound in relation to size that is so striking when listening to a wren.

Although the dipper's favourite haunt is such a stretch of stream as Isaak Walton fished, outside the breeding season it may be found on mere dribbles on the steep mountainside or, on Scottish islands, at the mouth of a stream, where it will feed at low tide among the shingle and seaweed. The dipper that breeds in Britain is distinguished from the continental race by having, below the white bib, a band of chestnut merging into the black of the belly. This area is wholly black in the Continental birds. These so-called black-bellied dippers frequently visit East Anglia in winter and may be seen on lowland streams, usually about a mill race, a weir, or other area of disturbed water.

In the drawing of the underside
the neck is extended while
in the drawing of the upper
surface it is relaxed thus
causing the difference in total
length in the two drawings.

The white of throat and chest was flecked
with sepia. According to Handbook this
indicates a first winter bird.

Tail (upper surface)

× 2½.

N.T.
♀ Dipper. From M. E. Davenport and obtained near
Monk's Heath, Cheshire. about Feb. 22ᵈ.
Wing. 92 mm.   Bill to Tail. 184 mm. (7¼″)

Ends of flights of closed
right wing

DIPPER *(Cinclus cinclus)*
'♀ Dipper. From M. E. Davenport and obtained near
Monk's Heath, Cheshire, about Feb. 22nd. Wing 93 mm. Bill
to tail 184 mm (7¼″). In the drawings of the underside the
neck is extended while in the drawing of the upper surface it
is relaxed thus causing the difference in total length between
the two drawings. The white of throat and chest was flecked
with sepia. According to the Handbook this indicates a first
winter bird.'

REDSTART

The redstart is a fairly common breeding bird in the hill country of the north and west of Britain but it is only sparsely distributed in the lowlands of the east and south and it is virtually absent from Ireland. It is a summer visitor and although it seems to favour the north and west it is by no means confined to hill country. It needs trees but is rarely found in the depths of a wood but rather about the edges. Areas of scattered trees such as parks and well-wooded gardens are sometimes occupied. On the higher ground it shuns open moorland and frequents the neighbourhood of farms with shelter-belts of trees and wooded gullies and valleys. The male in summer, as will be seen from Tunnicliffe's drawing, is much the more handsome bird, very striking with his dove-grey back, white forehead, black mask and bib and bright red underparts and tail. The female is dowdy by comparison but both share the red tail or *start* (cf. Start Point) which is constantly quivered up and down and, in display, is fanned into a vivid triangle and moved briskly from side to side. In winter the male is less splendid, the breeding finery being obscured by brown tips after the moult. These wear away, or are shed, as the breeding season approaches.

Redstarts are insect-eaters and are ever busy among the branches of trees, making fluttering fly-catching flights or darting to the ground to pick up some spied morsel. In autumn, when sometimes great numbers move down the east coast, often with pied flycatchers, the birds are more apt to feed on the ground but in general they are birds of the lower canopy of scattered trees.

The black redstart is a closely related species that is common on the Continent but breeds only sparsely in the south east of England. It favours rocks and walls rather than trees and made war-time news by breeding in some numbers on the bombed sites of London. It is scarcely known in Anglesey except rarely on passage and Tunnicliffe never obtained a specimen.

REDSTART (*Phoenicurus phoenicurus*)
Left hand figures:
'♀ Redstart. Obtained June 1st. Nth. Wales. Wing 73 mm.
Bill to tail 133 mm. approx.'

Right hand figures:
'♂ Redstart. Found at Sutton reservoir, East Cheshire, May
2nd by M.E.D. Drawn May 8th '65. Wing 78 mm. Bill to tail
133 mm.'

WHEATEAR

Opposite there is reproduced a sheet of drawings of no fewer than six wheatears. Tunnicliffe also made drawings of two other wheatears on separate sheets. These are not reproduced here.

Wheatears are summer visitors to Britain and are among the earliest to arrive. They are birds mainly of more remote uplands of the north and west but they are also found, albeit decreasingly, in the south and east, on sand-dunes, warrens, downs and cliff tops. They favour places of close sheep- or rabbit-cropped turf and usually with stone walls or tumbled rocks to provide nest sites and perches.

They are creatures of the ground and are rarely if ever seen in a tree or bush. Very active little birds, they are ever restlessly on the move, flitting from one slight eminence to another. They have a rather vertical stance but constantly bob and spread their striking black and white tails. As Tunnicliffe's drawings show there is much variation with sex and season in the colour and pattern of the head and body but the white rump and tail with a black inverted T-pattern is constant and unique among British birds.

The race that breeds in Greenland is commonly seen as it moves north in spring. It passes through the country in May, long after the British breeding birds have reached their nesting areas, and is slightly larger than the native birds and sometimes can be identified by the browner colouring of the males. One of Tunnicliffe's specimens is a Greenland wheatear.

Migrating wheatears used to be trapped extensively for food in the southern counties as they moved south over the downs. Willughby says they are called *wheatears* 'because at the time of wheat-harvest they wax very fat' but this is probably not the case. The word almost certainly has nothing to do with corn or with organs of hearing and is much more likely to be a reference to the bold patch of white on the rump and to be in fact a corruption of *white arse*. Wheatears do not eat wheat. They are insectivorous.

WHEATEAR (*Oenanthe oenanthe*)

'A. Greenland Wheatear. Obtained by R. Wagstaffe from near the canal at Hyde, East Cheshire. Sex not recorded. Wing 105 mm. Oct. 14th.

B. Wheatear. ♂ 1st winter. Obtained from M.E.D. Aug. 14th. Wing 92 mm.

C. ♂ Wheatear. From Reeve Edge Quarry, Cheshire–Derbyshire border. By M.E.D. 11th May '65. Wing 88 mm. Grey of breast probably grime picked up from the moors.

D. ♂ Wheatear. Obtained Sept. 6th from Eileen Wheeler. Picked up from the road in Anglesey. Much warmer in colour than bird B. Wing 95 mm. (Probably 1st winter)

E. 1st Summer ♂ Wheatear. E. Cheshire, May 28th. Wing 90 mm. Still much brown on lower back and scapulars. Wings and tail abraded. New tail feathers half grown.

F. ♂ Wheatear. 1st summer. May 20th. Axe Edge, Derbyshire. Much brown on upper surface. Lower back very brown. Wing 91 mm. Centre of breast pale grey.'

BLUE TIT

Tunnicliffe made a series of measured drawings of all the tits of Britain with the exception of the very local crested tit of the relict Caledonian forest and the bearded tit (if it be a tit) of extensive reed beds. We reproduce opposite the drawings he made of a cock blue tit that came from East Cheshire.

The blue tit scarcely needs introduction. It is widespread and common in the British Isles except for the far north of Scotland, the Outer Hebrides (where it is scarce) and Orkney and Shetland (where it is absent). It is primarily a bird of deciduous woodland but it is an adaptable and enterprising species and is found anywhere where there are trees, whether in woodland, parks, farmland or gardens. Although it is out-numbered there by the more specially adapted coal tit and (where it exists) the crested tit it is nevertheless common in coniferous woodland and has undoubtedly spread as a result of the extension of softwood forests in recent decades. It may also be found in some surprising and tree-less localities, for example in the depth of extensive reed-beds more proper to the bearded tit.

But it is well known because it is one of the most regular and persistent visitors to bird-tables, whether in city gardens, suburban gardens or in rural areas. Indeed it is *the* bird of the bird-table, *par excellence*. In its association with man it has developed a number of strange and inconvenient habits. The most familiar of these is its propensity for opening milk bottles and drinking the cream. This is now so universal that protective covering of milk bottles is almost everywhere necessary. It seems to have begun about 50 years ago and has rapidly spread wherever in Britain milk is delivered in this way. There has been much debate about the manner of this spread, whether it is a more or less simultaneous discovery by individual tits, or whether they learn primarily from one another. Less well known is the blue tit's practice in some areas of hacking out the putty from windows. Putty attacked is usually, but not exclusively, new putty in which the imperfectly hardened linseed oil may be supposed to be nourishing. Even more remarkable and disconcerting behaviour occurs occasionally when tits resolutely enter houses and tear wall-paper from walls and attack books, lampshades and the like, for no very clear reason.

Blue tits are very aggressive and pugnacious little birds, as will be found if a finger be inserted in a nest-box containing a sitting tit. Bewick remarked that 'This bird is distinguished above all the rest of the Titmice by its rancour against the owl'.

The word *tit* is an abbreviation of *titmouse* and until comparatively recently the official name for this and related birds was *titmouse*. The syllable *mouse* as nothing to do with mice but is an ancient Nordic word for a small bird. It appears as *Blaumeise* in German and similar words in other Teutonic languages. In the country the blue tit is often called the tomtit, an accolade of familiarity, Tom the tit, in the same way that *magpie* and *jackdaw* came respectively from Maggie the pie and Jack the daw.

Conspicuous pale nape when head is bent forward

Enlarged slightly.

enlarged

Right foot enlarged.

♂ Blue-tit. Obtained from M.J.R. East Cheshire. Dec. 16th 63. Wing 62mm. Bill to Tail. 4¼" (Monks Heath)

BLUE TIT (*Parus coeruleus*)
'♂ Blue Tit. Obtained M.J.R. Monk's Heath, East Cheshire, Dec. 16th '63. Wing 62 mm. Bill to tail 4¼". Conspicuous pale nape when head is bent forward.'

STONECHAT

Willughby's 'stone-smich or stonechatter or moor-titling' he says 'is found for the most part in Heaths, and is very querulous'. This is still true today, but the heaths are those, principally, of the coasts of Britain and more particularly those in the west of the country. It is believed that the bird was formerly more widespread but it is to a large extent resident (although some do migrate to the Continent in winter) and in severe weather the population is apt to be greatly reduced. This, and the tendency for suitable territory to disappear from inland regions, is thought to explain the bird's present coastal and westerly distribution. It is a very conspicuous bird, where present, from its habit of sitting exposed on the top of a gorse-bush, tall weed or fence post and constantly uttering its 'tack-tack' complaint, rather like, as Bewick quoting Latham says 'the clicking of two stones together, from which circumstance it probably derives its name'.

The stonechat has a very characteristic outline with a vertical stance, a rather large head and a short tail. The male in nuptial plumage with his black head, white flash on the neck and chestnut-pink breast is a very handsome bird. Tunnicliffe's bird (*opposite*) is a male obtained in Anglesey (where it is common) in October and at this season the black head is somewhat obscured by brown tips to the feathers which, as spring approaches, wear away to expose the glossy black of the breeding season.

A closely related species, the whinchat, is a summer visitor to Britain and thus escapes the severities of winter but nevertheless it also has declined in numbers in recent years particularly in the south and east of the country. Both species probably suffer from the decrease in undisturbed waste ground in rural areas resulting from the trimming of road verges, the tidying up of odd corners and the ploughing of marginal land. Whatever the reason the whinchat, like the stonechat, has become a relatively uncommon bird and is found mostly in upland areas of the north and west but without the coastal bias of the stonechat. Both species have been favoured by the extension of forestry plantations which, while the trees are small, provide suitable territory for both with rough vegetation and adequate song-posts and look-outs. The whinchat is the more likely beneficiary where the undergrowth is long grass. Stonechats seem to prefer heather or bracken with close-cropped grass.

STONECHAT (*Saxicola torquata*)
'♂ Stonechat. Obtained Oct. 22nd '66 from G.M. Anglesey.
Wing 66.5 mm.'

BRAMBLING

The splendidly decorative sheet (*opposite*) is composed of drawings of three bramblings, two females (*upper figures*) from Hampshire and (*below*) a male from Cheshire. The brambling is essentially a winter visitor to Britain from the Continent though a few pairs may breed from time to time in Scotland. It has a superficial resemblance to the chaffinch but is at once distinguished when a flock rises in flight and the white rump of the brambling becomes apparent. It moves about the country in flocks, often mixed with chaffinches, and feeds on seeds and grain of all sorts but seem to have a preference for beech mast. The buff tips to the upper head and back feathers of the male wear away, or are shed, by spring and these parts become a glossy black so that the breeding male brambling is a very distinguished bird.

In the Nordic countries, where it is a common breeding bird of birch and the edges of conifer forest as far north as the limits of the trees, it is known as the mountain finch.

BRAMBLING (*Fringilla montifringilla*)
'♀ Bramblings. From David Jenkins, Boro Down, Hampshire. Both birds (A and B) arrived March 1st. Probably obtained Feb. 26th or 27th.
Wing (A) 87 mm. Bill to tail (A) 6″ approx.
Wing (B) 90 mm. Bill to tail (A) 6⅛″ approx.
Tail feathers of this bird (B) were more pointed than those of bird A. There were also slight differences in the colour of the wing coverts.
♂ Brambling (C) obtained Gawsworth, East Cheshire, Nov. 22nd '66 by M.E.D. Drawn Nov. 28th.
Wing (C) 92 mm. Bill to tail (C) 152 mm. (6″).'

♀ BRAMBLINGS from David Jenkins, Bero Down, Hampshire. Both birds
arrived March 1ᵗ. Probably obtained Feb 26 to 29ᵗ.
Wing 87 mm. Bill to tail 6" approx.

Wing 90 mm. Bill to tail 6½" approx.
Tail feathers of this bird are more pointed than those
of bird A. There are also slight differences in the
colour of the wing coverts.

A. A. A.

B.

C. C. C.

×2

C.

♂ Brambling obtained Fanworth
East Cheshire Nov 22ⁿᵈ 66. by M E.D.
(Drawn Nov 28ᵗ)
Wing 92 mm. Bill to Tail 152 mm (6")

PARTRIDGE

The native partridge, sometimes called the common or grey partridge to distinguish it from the introduced red-legged partridge, is a widespread bird in Britain except for parts of Wales and the north and west of Scotland. It is, however, a much diminished species in recent years and over most of its range it is now scarce and in places the red-legged partridge is the more common bird. It is found in Anglesey and Tunnicliffe's specimen of which his drawings are reproduced opposite was shot in Newborough Warren. Indeed although it is a bird primarily of cultivated country it is commonly found on heaths and dunes and, although it is not found on high moorland, it is not infrequently present in moorland areas at the edge of cultivation.

The reasons for the reduction in the partridge population have been much debated and studied and it seems clear that modern farming methods are largely responsible. Although primarily vegetarian when adult it seems that the partridge when a chick needs an insect diet in order to thrive. This it used to get from the grassy 'headlands' and the hedgerows bordering arable fields which nowadays are subject to insecticidal sprays and in many districts have been entirely removed.

The word *partridge* is obviously derived from the Latin *perdix* and is doubtless a reference to the voice of the bird which used to be such a feature of arable country and has been well-likened to the turning of a key in a rusty lock. Perdix, of course, was cast from a tower by his jealous uncle Daedalus and saved and turned into a bird by Pallas Athene. So thenceforth he avoided high places and constantly uttered his name as a warning to others of his fate.

Willughby says, 'Partridges, to speak of them in general, are very salacious birds, infamous for masculine Venery, and other abominable and unnatural conjunctions'. He goes on to report from 'the Ancients' but adds, 'But it is not worth the while to insist long upon rehearsing or refuting these particulars'.

PARTRIDGE *(Perdix perdix)*
'♀ Partridge. 1st winter? Obtained Oct. 22nd '66,
Newborough Warren, by M.E.D. Wing 150 mm.

RED-LEGGED PARTRIDGE

The red-legged partridge is not a native British species, though Willughby says 'Howbeit they say it is found in the Isles of Jersey and Guernsey'. It was introduced deliberately from the Continent from about 1800 onwards and now occupies much of southern, eastern and central England. It is rather larger and is more boldly marked on the head and flanks than is the common or grey partridge (pages 150–151). Also it lacks the dark horseshoe mark on the underparts that characterises the grey species. The red-legged partridge does not occur in Anglesey and Tunnicliffe's bird came from a Manchester shop. In spite of attempts to introduce it to the north and west it has not become established in these areas of high rainfall. It does best where rainfall is low and the soil light and is particularly successful in East Anglia and in some parts is now more numerous than the native partridge. It seems less susceptible to the changes in farming practice that have been so detrimental to the grey partridge population and in parts of Norfolk where the former coveys of grey partridges are rarely seen the wheezing cough of the red-legged, or French, partridge is a common early summer sound.

Very different from the grey partridge in a close view, the red-legged partridge at a distance can look much like the native bird. It is rather more reluctant to take wing and although family parties feed together the coveys break up more readily and earlier in the season than do those of the grey partridge.

On the Continent it is found in southern France and in Spain but further east it is replaced by very similar species of the *Alectoris* genus, the rock partridge and the chukor. In North Africa yet another closely related bird, the Barbary partridge is found. All these species have a broadly similar basic pattern and differ only in detail and, most strikingly, in voice. Attempts to introduce the chukor into Britain have not so far been successful.

RED-LEGGED PARTRIDGE (*Alectoris rufa*)
'Red-legged partridge ♂. Bought in Manchester Shop Oct.
14th. All drawings life size exact. 12 red tail feathers and 2
brown feathers under coverts. Upper coverts extend beyond
the end of tail.'

C. F. TUNNICLIFFE
A Memoir

I went to live and work in Manchester in 1936. The work was interesting and the pay good in its day but to have to live there seemed like a term of imprisonment. Manchester then was a gloomy city of black buildings, tramlines and stone sets, drizzle and fog, and old grey women in grey shawls and clogs. There were more pleasing aspects. The concerts of the Hallé Society were accounted by some a major compensation. But not by me. My tolerance of Manchester stemmed from a delight in the ease of getting out of it and the glory of the surrounding countryside. To north, east and west the radiating roads took one through seeming endless forests of tall chimneys belching from the 'dark satanic mills' and the moors between were black and bleak. But to the south was Cheshire of green fields, pied houses and pied cattle. The East Cheshire hills of moorland and green valleys were not far away and beyond was Derbyshire, grand week-end walking country of gritstone and limestone hills and dales. Trains would take you quickly through to Cumbria or Caernarvonshire where there were veritable mountains, snow-capped in winter. And there were birds, some strange to the Midlander. The Cheshire meres had all manner of fowl; in the steep valleys to the east there were redstarts, on the moors were wheatears, curlew, golden plover and ring ouzel and about the hill streams dippers and grey wagtails were common. By train the Dee was easily reached and Hilbre Island was a fine place, where always in winter there were purple sandpipers and scoters and often a storm-driven oddity.

Then there was the Manchester Art Gallery with its superb collection of Pre-Raphaelite paintings and the annual exhibition of the Manchester Academy. Here one could ignore the soot and grime school, who, oddly enough, seemed to revel in dark streets, sombre skies, cotton mills and their chimneys, and black, soiled moorland. There were others who rejoiced, more explicably, in the pleasant surrounding country, the hills and dales, meadows and meres, the bright sunlight and the changing skies. There was also C. F. Tunnicliffe, an artist whose paintings were of the birds and animals of Cheshire in their natural setting. In effect landscape with figures but a diminutive landscape of no more than two or three square yards. Both

figures and setting were accurately observed and immaculately drawn. To a naturalist they were right. Moreover the composition, the pictorial design, the arrangement of figure and 'landscape' was always striking and harmonious, a careful and effective symphony in line, shapes, tone and colour.

I was enormously impressed and looked forward eagerly to the annual show of Tunnicliffe's paintings. I had been interested in birds and in drawing them as long as I could remember but in my teens the interest had been almost shed for the more practically useful and money-rewarding chemistry. These pictures were, I thought, what I myself might have done or, at least, would have liked to try to do.

In 1939 I married a girl from north Manchester whose parents had taken her, every year of her life, for several summer weeks, to a farm near Aberffraw in Anglesey. This lovely land of little sandy bays, dunes, rocks and low cliffs overlooked to the south a distant view of Welsh hills, stretching across the horizon from Carnedds and Glyders by Snowdon and lesser hills to the Rivals and the diminishing skyline of Lleyn. At night, afar, but nearer than the hills, Llanddwyn lighthouse shone, and in daytime too the white shape of the stubby tower could often be discerned. I borrowed a bicycle in Aberffraw and went to Newborough and walked in exploration over the warren to Llanddwyn Island.

At that time Llanddwyn, albeit an island only at the highest spring tides, was remote indeed. Newborough Warren had no road across its four miles from Newborough to Llanddwyn, only the vaguest of sandy tracks among the dunes. There was then but a very little recent conifer planting, in the corner nearest to Malltraeth, and the wild dunes were a flowery delight. Viper's bugloss in blue drifts, pink swathes of centaury, carpets of silverweed and *Viola curtisii* and little clumps, in damp places, of wintergreen and Grass of Parnassus. The 'island' was breeding home for a mixed colony of both arctic and common terns and a few pairs of the rare roseate tern; gulls bred on the cliffs; and on a reef beyond the lighthouse there was a colony of cormorants and shags, the cormorants making a frieze along its crest and the shags on ledges and in niches on the slopes. A few pairs of oystercatchers and ringed plovers were to be found feeding in the coves or feigning injury if you strayed too near their nests.

A very few human beings lived on the island. Two of a family called Jones. Mrs Jones, old and bent, daughter, widow and mother of successive light-house-keepers, cherished the birds for the R.S.P.B. Tom, her son, retired from the merchant fleet, looked after the lighthouse, caught lobsters and generally tended the island. Nelly, her daughter, lived in Newborough and daily crossed the warren on foot with Biddy the pack-donkey laden with provisions. There was also a white pony, Bess, and some kitchen-door fowls. There was a well of pure water. And there was a cottage to let. It was one of a row of four built for lifeboatmen. The remainder of the crew had been summoned from Newborough by the sound of cannon fire. But the lifeboat station was long gone to Caernar-von and the old iron cannon rusted muzzle-down on the cliff top. The cottage had two rooms downstairs, a living room and a double bedroom where mice scam-pered at night across the linen ceiling, and, in the loft, reached by a ladder from the living room, were two single beds. Just right for mum, dad and two small children. I took my family there every year for many years, sometimes several times. We were constantly enchanted. The view from the cottage door was unsurpassed: the sandy curve of Lifeboat Bay, the old ruined lifeboat house snug under the cliff crowned by the white landmark tower, the blue waters of Lland-dwyn Bay and beyond, the magnficent backcloth of Snowdonia and Lleyn. There were coves facing in several directions on the island so that there were few days when there was no sheltered, cosy beach. The cliffs were rugged but not very dangerous. Ruins of the abbey and two memorial crosses added interest. The even tenor of blissful days was disturbed only by such excitements as the arrival of a sailing boat to anchor in the bay and put a picnic party ashore; an exceptionally low tide exposing the mysteries of deeper weeds; the time when Abermenai beach was sprinkled with boat shells, never seen again; the grinning corpse of our only washed-up angler fish; the arrival of a host of velella or a huge rhysostome jelly-fish; the day when a grey seal joined our family in a morning swim in Lifeboat Bay; or when the lazy edge of the tide was the colour of tomato soup in the daytime and glowed eerily at night due to noctiluca.

If the island were not enough you could leave it and go for long walks. You could walk south towards Abermenai Point or north along Malltraeth beach, magnificent with breakers and backed by splendid dunes, or you could walk to Malltraeth village. Lland-dwyn Island is an extension of an outcrop of volcanic rock famous to geologists for its pillow lava and this forms a ridge of curious rock in the dunes from the island almost to Malltraeth. Now cloaked in pines it was then a bare steep rock ridge inhabited in the breeding season by herring gulls and ravens. You could follow this line over the warren or you could go round by Malltraeth Point where there was sometimes a large colony of terns. Short-eared owls, merlins and Montagu's harriers might be encountered in the dunes. A merlin occasionally appeared on Lland-dwyn, raiding for a meadow pipit. The harriers bred in those days in the sedge beds on the Cefni marshes. The Cefni estuary at low tide was a fine place for waders. At Malltraeth the estuary, many years ago, had had an embankment built across it called the Cob, with sluice gates by the village, to drain the marsh and control the tidal flooding. Upstream from the Cob was the Cob Lake, a long narrow brackish water between Cob and road. This lake was perhaps the richest and most varied bird place of all, especially in the early morning before the first of the traffic came along. Ducks of many kinds seemed to find it irresistible, pintail, shoveler, mallard, gadwall, teal, wigeon, smew, according to season, and often in considerable flocks. Herons and lapwing and snipe were usually there. Indeed there seemed no limit to what might turn up. Most winters there was a flock of 20 or more Bewick's swans. Once a spoonbill fed among the mute swans of May. In April there were usually garganey, splendidly red black-tailed godwits and, flitting by the lake and running along the wall tops, little groups of migrant white wagtails. But this is not a natural history of south-west Anglesey. Enough has perhaps been said to show it as a lonely, beautiful and bird-rich locality. It was to this delightful spot that I became a regular visitor just after the war and to which Charles Tunnicliffe, about the same time, came to live.

At that time I had not met him. We had corres-ponded when he lived in Macclesfield, at Hurdsfield. I had sent him samples of my Sunday work and asked for critical commentary and even for his support for my membership of the Manchester Academy. His letters to an importunate stranger had been kindly, forthright and helpful – and brief. One day I was bird-watching by the Cob Lake and a large, jovial and ragged man in an old car drove by, stopped and spoke to me. We talked for a while before I remembered that I had heard recently that Tunnicliffe had gone to live in Anglesey and I realised that this was he. He didn't deny it. He had a sketchbook, binoculars and a fine telescope. He had been drawing ruffs and reeves. So had I. But mine might have been redshanks or godwits; his were unmistakeable. He told me just what it was about a ruff's facial 'expression' that makes it a ruff and nothing else. He invited me to his house that afternoon to meet Winifred, his wife, and to have a cup of tea and see his studio.

His new home, Shorelands, was a bungalow on the north shore of the estuary. The front room was his studio. It had a large bay-window overlooking an S-bend in the Cefni as it wended at low tide from the gates in the Cob across the sands to the sea. Beyond the sands was Newborough Warren, then just beginning to be clad in alien pines, and beyond that the noble skyline of the mainland of North Wales. The room faced south, not the conventional direction for an artist's studio, but the intrusive sun was controlled by Venetian blinds and the greenhouse temperature of summer was dealt with by working clad only in shorts and sandals. It was a practical workshop, devoid of comfort or elegance, with large Edwardian bookcases and cupboards and with easels and work-tables littered with the painter's paraphernalia. He showed me his sketchbooks, at that time worked in pencil and ink and coloured crayons. Tea was served in a sitting-room of fine furniture, carved by Winifred. She was Irish, bonny, dryly humorous and efficient. I was asked to call again whenever I was in Anglesey and I did; several times a year until we left the neighbourhood of Manchester, more rarely in later years from East Anglia. The Tunnicliffes became firm friends and a visit to Anglesey always included a visit to Shorelands. Most visits were brief calls late in the day when work was over, for tea and talk. But sometimes they would take a day off and walk over to Llanddwyn to see us, or invite us to join an outing to favourite haunts near Cemlyn, Llugwy, Moelfre or Dulas. Sometimes when surrogate parents could be found Mary and I would spend a week-end in Anglesey in winter-time and Charles and Winifred would eat with us at the Joiner's Arms in Malltraeth, just across the road from Shorelands.

Though I was never with him continuously for more than half a day and was in no sense his pupil, in so long an acquaintance I learnt a great deal about him and his working methods. He was always ready to answer questions though the answers were often waggish and indirect. When I remarked on his use of wax crayons in his sketches, an unusual medium, he said one should use anything that came to hand that would produce the right effect: pencil, pen and ink, chalk, crayon, transparent watercolour, gouache – 'soot from the chimney or spit'. He professed no regard for purity of medium, nevertheless his exhibition paintings were essays in transparent water colour with skilful use of masking fluid and an occasional knife scratch. Asked about the paper he used he was always vague and apparently uncertain. He had a large stock and selected with care a sheet most suitable for the job in hand without always knowing the name of the paper he used. He often resorted to a tinted paper. I have a painting of an eagle owl on a buff paper, the paper colour being used as a ground colour for the bird; and another of birds in the rain on a grey paper which tones down all whites and effectively suggests the sombre light of downpour. He was insistent on the importance of design and com-

position. Observing that a page in a sketchbook could make a picture: 'Yes, and it will, if I can get a good arrangement'. Did he arrive at a 'good arrangement' by instinct and feeling, or did he follow rules of composition such as the Golden Section? No, of course he didn't observe rules or work by mathematics – 'but a knowledge of these things is helpful'.

What about detail? One noticed that the measured life-size records were drawn and painted with careful exactitude, whereas in the exhibition works detail, while always skilfully 'suggested', was not meticulously 'painted'. Here he would be expansive. A picture should have regard to the purpose for which it was painted and the normal distance at which it was to be viewed. An illustration for a book to be held in the hand called for different treatment from a picture to decorate a wall. A large painting on a wall would not normally be viewed more closely than the distance at which the eye could embrace the whole picture. Detail invisible at that distance was labour wasted – and indeed labour to a disadvantage, for excessive working was bound to sully hues and obscure tonal pattern. Asked how he devised the pattern of brush-marks that so convincingly, at the proper viewing distance, suggested complex ripples on water, a clump of catmint or a patch of flowering grass dew-laden, he said 'Get an odd scrap of paper and try and try again until you get a recipe; then use it'.

He had little regard for most contemporary painters of birds and animals, nor much for the great illustrators. His gods were the Chinese, the Swede Liljefors, Crawhall. Producing, as he did, paintings whose splendour lay in the recording of real life, in a convincingly captured moment observed, what did he think of Van Gogh, Gauguin, the Fauves, more 'modern' painters? He was, to me then, surprisingly tolerant, even worshipful. Indeed one came to see in his colour patterns, his juxtapositions of hue and tone, the influence especially of Gauguin and Matisse. For most painters of natural history subjects these artists might never have lived. For Tunnicliffe they were an inspiration and an example. 'Always, up to now, I've let the bird make the pattern. One of these days, my lad, I shall let the pattern make the bird!' But he never did, his regard for the realities of nature observed kept him in the 'representational' category, a kind of painter art critics of the day fashionably decry – or ignore. It would be wrong to regard his struggles with failing eyes and hands very late in life as anything other than the losing battle they were.

I do not recollect his remarking on it but a study of the design of his paintings will often reveal an essay in point and counterpoint: a displaying turkey's spread tail echoed by a rusting old cart-wheel and similar conjunctions, sometimes obvious, more frequently subtle and even obscure, but always one of the keys to the satisfaction that contemplation of his pictures affords. He was most pleased with a picture in which he had reached, besides a skilfully faithful representation of animal or bird and its surroundings, also a careful and subtle abstract design. He did occasionally make pictures by direct transference of something seen, almost regardless of composition; but he never had the same regard for these works as for those where the design satisfied his exacting standard.

Charles Tunnicliffe was, of course, unlike so many of us who presume to draw and paint birds and animals, a fully and thoroughly trained artist. There was no question of 'I can't draw ... this or that'. As any worthy artist can he could draw anything. He had no sympathy for the absurd concept that a bird painter might be a good bird painter and yet bad with other subject matter. His draughtsmanship was superb. He was skilled in many techniques. Not only was he a fine draughtsman and a splendid painter in watercolours, he was also a good painter in oils, an accomplished etcher, a distinguished wood-engraver, and a sound exponent of scraper-board technique. By the time I knew him he had given up etching and was almost at the end of his career as a wood-engraver. I think for two reasons: he undoubtedly found the delicate work entailed by such techniques a strain on his eyesight in middle age. But also the demand for illustrative work was increasingly tending towards the quicker and cheaper scraper-board drawing. He had for a number of years exhibited with the Royal Society of Painter-Etchers and Engravers and his exhibit at the Royal Academy had often included fine wood engravings. But in the last few decades of his life his exhibited work had become almost exclusively watercolours, both at the Royal Academy and in his occasional one-man shows at the Tryon Gallery. Although he remained a member of the Manchester Academy he had ceased to exhibit there in, I think, the mid-50s. His drawings in black and white were done almost exclusively for the illustration of books. For this work he was in constant demand, particularly by certain authors and publishers. His relatively few works in oils were painted usually to commission, though he painted a few landscapes to decorate his own living-room; it was unusual to see bird or animal paintings in his house. No matter how favourite, they were all sold.

He had two main sources of information for his work, firstly his sketchbooks and secondly his measured drawings, made life-size, exactly measured, from the dead specimens that came into his hands. The sketchbooks were in constant use, both as source material and as repositories for new observations. They were not, I think, for the most part used in the 'field' but the drawings were made while memory was fresh as soon as he returned to the studio from a spell of observation. Very rough notes were made separately in the 'field' itself. The sketchbooks might contain a very detailed drawing of a bird that had permitted close observation or they might have pages of tiny sketches of postures in perching, feeding, preening or flying; rapid movements uncannily noted by long practice and, above all, there was never a note of what he knew he ought to see – only of what he actually did see; a very wholesome and necessary exercise in self-discipline for some of us! I remember once his showing me a sketch of a gyrfalcon that had perched briefly on a post in the estuary some distance from his studio window. 'Why didn't you put a bit more in'? I asked, 'Because that was all I could see'.

I suppose he rarely painted an exhibition picture for which he had not a sheaf of sketch notes and one or more measured drawings. The sketchbooks ensured accuracy in his figures of stance and posture, of what the bird-watcher calls the 'jizz', and very often suggested design and composition. They also contained notes of water, sand ripples, stones, plants or whatever were to be used in the setting. The measured drawings served to give accuracy to necessary detail, to fill in gaps in memory and sketches. But if asked to draw a bird or animal for which he lacked this material he would use any source to hand, visits to zoos, photographs, museum mounts, study skins, anything. I remember being at his studio once when he was painting a fox and cubs in oils; he had pinned on a board all the photographs of foxes, in whatever pose, that he had collected over the years; and the painting bore no resemblance to any of them. But he always emphasised that all sources must be taken with a grain of salt – even one's own sketches, for memory is fallible. Only his measured drawings were beyond argument and they were no help in drawing the living posture. Black and white photographs confused light and shade with light and dark colours; colour photographs reproduced colour inexactly; all photographs were apt to fix atypical poses; skins faded and dead limbs shrivelled; the sausage shapes of museum skins were good only for feather detail but deceptive in the relationship of one feather to the other; mounts depended in frailty on the taxidermist's art. All were fallible but none need be despised, if treated with proper reserve. But the essence of natural history art was to draw from life, and draw from life again, to observe, to memorise and to know. His best pictures were of those subjects of his constant acquaintance: cows, cats, horses, lapwings, pintails, black-headed gulls and mallard; falcons and owls; the common birds and animals of his life in Cheshire and of that little heavenly corner of Anglesey that latterly he had made his home. 'I haven't finished with black-headed gulls yet', I remember he remarked on one of our later meetings.

He rarely emerged from Anglesey. He was always busy working because he was asked to work or because he wanted to work. It was all one. When he and Winifred went on holiday it usually entailed work. To Islay or Iona or Sutherland to draw deer or diver, tystie, otter or fulmar. He poured a detached and contemplative scorn on the current pull-devil-pull-baker of modern industry, of organised pressure for less work and more pay. Hours mattered little so long as there was daylight to work in. Winifred helped in a truly co-operative enterprise. She it was, before she fell mortally ill, who went to see agents and publishers, framers and galleries, conducted business correspondence and ran the household. Occasionally she made the measured drawings when pressure of other work kept him from a rapidly ripening corpse. He had a special dispensation from the Royal Academy that he be excused attendance at their affairs. I used, when I first knew him, and in my blindness, to invite him to stay with us and to attend with us the Manchester Academy Conversazione. He never came. He probably regarded us, privily and at times, as a bit of a nuisance. He certainly had little use, indeed he said as much, for the bird sentimentalists who called on him. 'A couple of years spreading muck' was the remedy he suggested. Of the earth, earthy; brought up on a farm, he had no use for the slushy regard for animal life. We are carnivores and must eat. Pig-killing is as much, or was as much, a part of village life as the planting of potatoes. His early etchings recorded it in all its squealing, bloody, savage ritual. He loved the spectacle of fox-hunting and would have liked to go to Spain to see a bullfight – and to paint it. Unnecessary cruelty was abhorrent but it was better to wring a bird's neck than to waste time in cossetting the irreparable. But he could be heartily contemptous of the idle free-lance marsh shooter-at-anything who shot a glossy ibis in the 'belief' that it was a curlew – and not forgive him even if the ibis found its way into his collection of measured drawings!

He was a friendly, jovial, witty man; coarse and yet delicate; uncouth yet refined; hearty, humorous, jolly; a grand teller of a tale; without conceit but full of pride in his work; always pleased to see us. 'And how are the chips'? came in the first few remarks. 'Off the old block-head' he had long ago explained. The air, the light, the smell of Anglesey will not fade in my mind, nor the sound of his voice and his laughter. An upbringing on a small mixed farm, a fondness for Cheshire meres, an abiding affection for Malltraeth, for the Cefni marshes, for Llanddwyn, and that odd desire to put things down on paper, all these we had in common, in spite of far divergences in our lives; and it was enough to make for a mutual regard and affection that it hurts to recollect in the realisation that it has gone.

As the years pass no place on earth is the same, or seems the same, or as good, as it used to seem. It is certainly so to me in that corner of Anglesey. The S-bend in the river at low tide outside the studio window at Shorelands has been straightened. The sluice gates at Malltraeth have been 'improved'. The traffic along the road has much increased and birds no longer frequent the Cob Lake as much as they used to do. The pine trees have become a tall pine forest that quite conceals the dunes. The Forestry Commission has made a metalled track through the forest so that cars may pass and the formerly lonely beaches of Abermenai and Malltraeth are thronged with man and his mate, their young, their litter and their noise. The Nature Conservancy, in its fashion, 'preserves' Llanddwyn; but it is a dead island, no Biddy or Bess, no Jones and no tern, no merlin nor any Montagu's harrier. None may live there unless they be scientists to ring and weigh, to count and measure, in the name of the currently fashionable jargon, ecology.

And Charles and Winifred are now both dead. The hills and the sea remain and so do Charles' water-colours. He was not a man of great learning but one of accomplished and profound knowledge. Knowledge not only of the way of an eagle in the air and the way of a man with a maid but knowledge of the intimate character of animals and birds, of the way a puff of wind lifts feathers, of the way shallow waters ripple and sparkle, how the sea breaks onshore in a pattern of sand and foam, how waves run down from rocks in runlets of lace, how dew lies on grass, raindrops on twigs, hoar frost on reeds, and the sun on a falcon's back; how a bird crouches head to the wind, how it struggles to retain its stance in a changing gust, how fallen leaves blow and cock's feathers glisten, how cats play and otters swim. Knowledge indeed from a lifelong habit of noting with his own special eye the peculiarly and delightfully decorative elements in the smaller features of the natural world. Perhaps he has enabled some of us to see pattern and decoration and beauty in the little things surrounding us and to delight in what might otherwise have been hidden.

PICTURE INDEX